Hey John.
Hey God.

What Happens When God Writes Back

John Roedel

John Roedel
Cheyenne, WY 82001
www.heygodheyjohn.com

Book Layout © 2017 BookDesignTemplates.com

Hey God. Hey John. / John Roedel – 1st edition.

ISBN-13: 978-1720783077
ISBN-10: 1720783071

For my Jenni,
who believes
in me enough
for the both
of us.

Contents

Waiting For An Answer

"I'm waiting for your answer, Mister Roedel," Miss Millhop said to me impatiently.

I looked up at my seventh-grade religion teacher desperately trying to read her gaze for a clue to the particular answer that she waiting for me to give. Miss Millhop's hard stare offered zero help. After a few moments of awkward silence she crossed her arms tightly across her chest, her rosary gripped tightly between her fingers, dangling back and forth in front of me like a hypnotist's stopwatch.

In my entire academic career at Catholic school, Miss Millhop was the only teacher I encountered who enjoyed weaponizing her faith and deploying it against as many puberty-stricken teens as she could. Every class she would wrap up Jesus in a thick shield of barbed wire and scare us about the probability that none of us would ever be worthy of His love. Miss Millhop taught Catholicism in the same manner that an army drill sergeant would teach proper grenade handling. Religion class was life or death. *If you don't pay attention to everything that I'm telling you, there is a 100% chance that you will be sorry.* "Being sorry" didn't mean having your arm blown off by a poorly thrown frag grenade. No, it meant something far worse:

Hellfire.

I'm pretty sure that in my three years under Miss Millhop's rule I was promised that I would taste the sulphury flames of hell approximately five hundred times.

About two minutes earlier Miss Millhop had caught me at work on a doodle featuring her being eaten by some large and hungry alien. After disposing of my edgy piece of modern art she came back to my desk to deliver her usual public shaming for having drifted off into my imagination during one of her terrifying lectures.

She demanded in front of the entire class what it was I thought God wanted from me...

I had an answer in mind, but I was sure that it would only incite further fury from Miss Millhop, who was far too young to be so angry all the time. Her dress was funereal on black with a hint of purple, just to make sure everyone knew that she celebrated Lent all year long.

"Well?" she asked. "Are you ready to give the class your answer, Mister Roedel?" I hated it when she called me that. It made it sound like she was a salty District Attorney and I was a meaty scumbag under her cross-examination. I shrugged my shoulders to signify that I was ready to surrender, which stirred her into a rage.

My tormentor's jaw was clenched so hard that I almost expected her to spit out a couple of molars on my desk. I seemed to represent the antithesis of Miss Millhop's philosophy of life. Her mission was to impress on her pupils the likelihood of their burning in hell; I believed in eating Starbursts and sneaking out of bed at night to watch The Love Boat.

She lurched down over me, her rosary thrust in front of my face.

"Not good enough! Give your answer! What is it that you think God wants from you?"

I looked at my friend, Dan who was sitting next to in desperation. He didn't look at me and I didn't blame him. Nobody wants to jump on a sinking boat.

Miss Millhop was growing impatient.

"Don't look at him, Mister Roedel. Someday God will judge you and your friends won't be able to bail you out. Someday you will face the lake of fire all on your own."

This was all well-trodden ground. We had performing this routine together all year. If I wanted this exchange to come to an end, I would have to apologize for my lack of respect and attention.

"Do you have something to say?" she asked.

This was my cue for an insincere "sorry" for not paying attention to her lengthy sermon of brimstone and fear.

"I think God wants me to be happy," I said.

This finally unhinged Miss Millhop. Not a screaming, rageful kind of unhinged, but in cackles of hysterical laughter. Looking back, I believe this may have been the first time she had laughed in decades and it was hard to know if she or the class was more shocked.

"You fool! God doesn't care about your happiness! God is only concerned with your obedience and absolute faithfulness. You don't know the first thing about how to follow God."

She was right then and she remains right thirty years later.

I have never known how to follow God.

I realize that sentiment isn't exactly what you expect to hear from somebody who publishes his conversations with God for thousands of people to read on Facebook, but it's true. I'm a spiritual mess. For me, having faith in God is like trying to catch a salmon in a wide Wyoming river with just my small hands. Believing in the unseen with conviction has been a practice that continues to elude me. Just when I think I have a firm grasp on a relationship with God, the whole thing slips through my hands and I find myself alone with only my doubts.

Understanding the nature of God has become as frustrating to me as trying to put together a giant puzzle in a dark room. Sometimes I think I have found all of the edges, only to discover more pieces that need to fit somewhere. My crisis of faith baffles and maddens me. I've long marveled at people who have a faith so deep that they can speak with complete certainty about God, whereas I am a bumbling detective looking for clues to the great mystery of spirituality.

For most of my life I have faked having a relationship with God. When I was a child I followed the spiritual breadcrumbs that were laid out for me by my parents. It all felt hollow to me. I attended a Catholic school and spent my time locking horns with the likes of Miss Millhop. I went to church, but lip-synched all of the hymns and whispered the "Our Father" at night with less enthusiasm than I had for eating my greens.

Age and experience did nothing to resolve my crisis of faith. I have visited iconic spiritual locations around the world and felt nothing but the creeping pain of disbelief. Worse, I worked in youth ministry and hid all of my doubts behind a mask of fake smiles and flowery words. I felt like such a fraud – and I still do.

My doubts are not just in God. They are also in me.

I have always believed in God. The thing is, I have long held the suspicion that God has stopped believing in me – not that I could blame Him for that. I lost faith in myself somewhere in my early twenties. My childhood was as easy as anybody could wish for. My parents loved and indulged me and gave me every opportunity to succeed. Nothing was hard for me. Aside from losing my right eye in an accident when I was seven, the first act of my life was like a gentle saunter down a freshly paved road.

The potholes came when I reached adulthood. Here are the highlights:

On the day I was planning on telling my dad that I was moving to Chicago to pursue a career in comedy, he called and told me that he had lung cancer. He asked if I would be willing to move back home and help him and my mother out. I agreed and put that dream on the back burner, where it has remained ever since.

Our first-born son was diagnosed at the age of two with autism. My combination of self-centeredness & cowardice meant that I was ill-equipped to deal with the challenge.

I watched both of my parents die a decade apart from each other.

My family's 118-year-old drugstore was forced to close on my watch.

My response to these challenges was to fall into a dark depression that felt like I was trapped at the bottom of a deep well.

The older I became and the more potholes I faced, the more complicated my relationship with God has grown. Over the course of a decade I quit talking to God altogether. The collapse of our relationship felt like a slowly melting ice cube in my hand. Little by little my sense of God slipped through my fingers until I was left with nothing but spiritual frostbite and a numb heart.

Eventually, my numbness turned into anger and the conviction that God had abandoned me. I felt like I was going through all of my suffering alone. God didn't save my parents or our family business. God didn't spare my child from autism or me from my depression. I felt like I was drowning in the terrible storm my life had become.

One day, about two and a half years ago I began to write peevish little posts that began with "Hey God." on Facebook, where I would have fake conversations with the Almighty. It was my attempt to put into words my frustrations with being an imperfect human living in a world supposedly created by a divine being. As a theological buffoon and the worst possible evangelist God could hope for, this whole project was born with some serious disadvantages to it. The first hundred posts were mostly ridiculous and trite, but then something happened:

I started to tether myself to these posts.

I began to write about subjects like our family's experience with autism, my deepening faith crisis, society's addiction to breaking news and my own journey into the dark woods of depression.

The more I wrote about these serious issues, the better I felt and the more grounded I became. My simple dialogues gave voice to the monsters under my bed that had been begging to be heard.

I started planning my days around my posts. I began to plan ahead. I trained my mind to focus on what I would write tomorrow or next week.

I would have continued to post these therapeutic missives for myself, even if all of my readers had grown tired of them and defriended me. That didn't happen. Over time my readers began to share my posts with their friends and I decided to start my own blog page called "Hey God. Hey John."

Since then the blog has continued to grow beyond the point where I could think of it as just a "fun little experiment", despite my many attempts to quit or sabotage myself. A thousand posts, 365 thousand words and 14 thousand Facebook followers later, my heart began to open to the possibility that maybe my words had real meaning behind them, a prospect that still terrifies me.

The last thing I want to do is to act like I am something that I am not, so, let me be clear on a couple of things.

Over the last few years I have received messages from readers asking me if I actually believe that writing Facebook posts is a form of prayer. I know this isn't the traditional way of communicating with our Maker. When I type God's responses I am writing exactly what my heart needs to hear at that exact moment. God says to me exactly what I would hope God would say to me if we were sitting down having tea.

So it begs the question: "Is this actually the real voice of God?"

Who knows?

I don't think God uses Facebook and is writing me back while sipping on a white mocha latte. If I were to guess, I think God could find people a lot more qualified than I am for such public discourse. I am neither a theological scholar nor a spiritual mystic, and I'm certainly not someone with all of the answers. Rather I am the sort of guy who burns microwave popcorn and routinely leaves the television remote control in the fridge. I am not an evangelist who has more certainty than faith. The truth is that I am a hot mess who hasn't worn matching socks for decades.

It begs the question of where do I get the answers that God gives in our conversations? I honestly don't know. Is it a collected wisdom that a part of my brain has accumulated over the years? I would be surprised if that were the case because I am unable to commit anything other than 90s music trivia and one recipe for really fabulous chicken curry to my long-term memory (see the end of the book for the recipe). Very often the responses that God comes up with in these posts are a revelation to me. There are times when I can't believe the words that appear as my fingers bash the keyboard. So, is this God actually talking with me, or is this just the manifestation of some inner wisdom that I never knew I possessed? I think it can be both of those things. The only thing I know is that the advice that God gives me is the exact words that I need to read in that moment.

I am the last person you would expect to write a book like this. Seriously. Maybe that is exactly why the both of us need to read it.

This book is a transcript of my never-ending crisis of faith that I have been sharing on

Facebook for the past few years and, as I look back on it, I have started to see a shift in my personal experience of spirituality. While I don't think that I am that much closer to achieving inner peace or blind faith than I was on the day that I started, post by post I see that my heart has softened a little more each time I "spoke" with God.

These conversations with God have pushed me to ask questions or broach topics that I was too scared to talk about with anybody else.

Even after all of these conversations I still can't quite answer the question of what it is that God wants from me, but I am excited for the journey I am on. Every day I wake up and sit down at my keyboard and, with God's help, little by little I am pushing open that wooden door in my heart.

I hear the ghost of Miss Millhop standing right behind me whispering in her cold voice.

"I'm still waiting for your answer Mister Roedel..."

Me too, lady. Me too.

How to read this book

One of the most challenging parts of putting this book together is trying to figure out how to organize it. When sitting down to write my first "Hey God. Hey John." post three years ago I never considered that this would become a book, which means that I didn't plan on any specific sort of flow or structure to it. At first I thought about putting it in chronological order to show the progression of my spiritual journey, which seemed a bit self-centered and not at all the aim of this book. Then I tried to impose a structure by arranging the posts thematically, but didn't want to overwhelm my readers with a dozen posts about depression in a row that would have them running for a gallon of chocolate ice cream.

After spending some serious time in prayer and hand-wringing I have decided to arrange the posts into four distinct parts that help show that the more I availed myself to God, the deeper the posts and my spiritual experience have become. In reflection, I have noticed a definite arc to what has been happening in my heart. You won't be reading these posts in strict chronological order or in compartmentalized themes like "Grief" or "Mental Health" or "Carpe Diem" but in four acts:

Act I: Hey God, remember me?

Act II: Hey God, this is getting weird.

Act III: Hey God, I can't do this alone.

Act IV: Hey God, I surrender.

From my first posts in which I spent time complaining to God about the lack of waffles in my life, to my later posts where I found myself penning spiritual poetry, my experience writing "Hey God. Hey John." has taken me on an incredible faith journey that has transformed my life. The decision to put the book together in this manner isn't meant to be braggadocious. For someone who at least once a year accidently brushes his teeth with anti-itch cream and still can't figure out how to drive a car with a stick shift, there isn't much for me to crow about. My hope is that this collection of my posts about my spiritual adventure will demonstrate that if even a schlub like me can find a way to develop my spirituality, anybody can.

I'm not a mystic or a spiritual guru. I'm just a guy who showed up daily to God with an open heart and an open Facebook page. Do you remember the movie Ratatouille? It is a lovely film about a rat that trains to become a master chef in a fancy Parisian restaurant. The moral of the movie that Disney hit us on our heads over and over with their trademarked velvet hammer was that "Anybody can cook!" – even a rat. That is what my journey has been about. If a guy like me can rebuild his relationship with God, then anybody can. Even you.

How should you read this? However you want to! Whatever works best for you is exactly how you should proceed. My only advice is that you should try to forget about me as you read it. I don't want this to be my story with God. I want it to be yours. Replace the "John" in all of the conversations with your own name.

Maybe you are like me and you have lost your way spiritually.

Maybe you have also fallen out of relationship with God.

Maybe you also doubt that God can actually hear you.

Maybe you also question your purpose in this world.

Maybe you also struggle with mental illness.

Maybe you also don't know how long you can hold on.

Maybe you also have that voice in your head telling you to be afraid of God.

Maybe you are also looking for something to spark you to believe in your dignity again.

Maybe this book is about our journey back to faith.

Maybe I wrote this for the both of us.

Put yourself in the "Me" of every entry and see where it leads your heart.

Allow God to show you something beautiful.

ACT I:
Hey God, do You remember me?

I started typing notes to God
on Facebook as a way
of poking fun at my crisis of faith.
At first it was all just for entertainment...but
then something happened:
God wrote back.
I was just messing around.
Turns out that God wasn't.

"Ah please talk to me
Won't you please talk to me
We can unlock this misery
Come on, come talk to me"
—Peter Gabriel

A Spark

Me: Hey God.

God: Hey John.

Me: What is this?

God: This is us talking.

Me: Or is it just me talking to myself?

God: Nope. I'm here.

Me: What if You aren't there?

God: I am.

Me: How am I supposed to know?

God: Take My word for it.

Me: You mean take my word for it...since I'm just talking to myself here.

God: Have faith.

Me: Easy for You to say.

God: Eventually you'll see Me.

Me: When?

God: When the time is right.

Me: That is a little vague.

God: That's because I'm just so mysterious.

Me: I hate mysteries.

God: You're going to have to get used to it. Mystery surrounds you.

Me: What if these conversations are a sign that I'm going crazy?

God: Then at least you'll be able to get that lobotomy your parents always predicted you'd have someday.

Me: Super.

God: Just keep talking to Me.

Me: Why?

God: So, neither of us are lonely.

Me: What do you want to talk about?

God: Everything.

Me: Everything it is.

Waffles

Me: Hey God.

God: Hey John.

Me: I'm going to pray.

God: Great! It's been a long time.

Me: Are you ready?

God: Go for it.

Me: I want waffles.

God: I think you have Me confused with room service.

Me: Make sure to bring some extra syrup up with them. I like to see how much maple syrup I can consume before I start hallucinating.

God: You should try praying for other people.

Me: You think I should pray for somebody else?

God: Yep.

Me: I pray that somebody will bring me some waffles.

God: I'm taking the rest of the day off.

Mistaken Identity

Me: Hey God.

God: Hey John.

Me: I thought you'd like to know that I started following your advice.

God: Great! Which piece of advice was that?

Me: It was the talk about how I need to start focusing on myself more and to quit wasting my time worrying about helping other people. I'm putting John first in 2015!

God: Wait a second, that doesn't sound like Me at all. That sounds like the exact opposite of what I would say.

Me: Huh. I wonder who told me that then.

God: I have no idea but they sound selfish.

Me: Oh yeah, I remember who told me that. It was me!

God: Of course it was.

Me: I get You and me mixed up sometimes.

God: That sounds about right.

Expanding The Universe

Me: Hey God.

God: Hey John.

Me: Thanks for meeting me at Perkins.

God: No worries. I love their senior discount. Why are you smiling?

Me: I am in such a good mood!

God: That's cool.

Me: Yeah, I'm really kicking some butt today and being super productive.

God: Great!

Me: I love the feeling that comes with finishing a huge project.

God: Did you finish writing that book that you started ten years ago?

Me: Uh, no. I need a little more time on that one...

God: Then what are you so happy about?

Me: Oh well, I woke up this morning and my dog had a bunch of poop stuck in his fur and –

God: Gross. I shouldn't have asked a follow-up question.

Me: You're going to be happy you did because I was able to give him a full bath without flooding the entire bathroom and first floor of our house this time!

God: And?

Me: And? And I'm awesome!! Woo hoo!

God: So, your measure of being productive is successfully scrubbing feces out of your dog's coat?

Me: Yes!

God: You may be setting the bar a little low for yourself these days.

Me: What do you mean?

God: I thought you were going to say that you found a job or something.

Me: Uh, no. I need a little more time on that one...

God: Like the book?

Me: Yes, like the book. Your tone seems a bit sarcastic.

God: I'm God, I don't have a tone. Look, John, if you are happy, then I'm happy. Good job on giving your poopy dog a bath. I mean it.

Me: Thanks! Enough about me. What have you been up to this morning?

God: Not much. Just forming seven new galaxies and creating stars from nothingness. You know, stuff like that.

Me: When did you get started doing that? Earlier this morning?

God: No. I'm literally expanding the universe while I'm talking to you. Oops. I'm now up to eight galaxies. Would you like me to name one after you?

Me: No...

God: What's wrong?

Me: You're kind of a one-upper.

Let's Talk About Something Else

Me: Hey God.

God: Hey John.

Me: My toenails are growing abnormally fast. Why do you think that is?

God: Of all the things we need to discuss, this is what you want to talk about?

Me: Yep.

God: Fine. Your toenails are growing at a rapid pace because you are a mutant and are about to undergo your final metamorphosis and turn into the superhero you always thought you would be.

Me: No wonder I love wearing tights! It all makes sense now.

God: Professor X should be contacting you soon to begin your training.

Me: Yes!!

God: I'm kidding, of course.

Me: Dang!

God: Your toenails aren't growing any faster than normal. You just haven't cut them in a long time.

In fact, according to my records the last time you trimmed them was back in May of 2011.

Me: They're hard to reach! Would you mind cutting them for me?

God: Sorry. That is not going to happen.

Me: Why?

God: I only help those who help themselves.

Me: How can I help myself cut them when you gave me dinosaur arms?? I can't even reach the tops of my feet to shave them.

God: You're shaving the tops of your feet now?

Me: I'm interested in leading a body-hair-free lifestyle.

God: Seriously, is this what we are talking about today? Don't you ever get tired of talking about yourself all the time?

Me: No. What else is there to talk about?

God: Anything sounds better than the topic of your toenails and fuzzy body.

Me: Well...let's see. We never talk about you. How about that?

God: Me?

Me: Sure. There are things that I would love to know about You.

God: Great! What would you like to know?

Me: How old are you?

God: I am older than time itself.

Me: I don't think that makes any sense.

God: Sure, it does. Just close your eyes and imagine the beginning of time. Now imagine that I was around before that.

Me: I'm not sure how that works mathematically.

God: I am math.

Me: That's a confusing statement. Um, okay, let's try something else. Describe what your home looks like?

God: You mean Heaven?

Me: Sure. What does it look like?

God: Alright. Well, for starters it is the essence of all light that has ever existed or ever will.

Me: I'm looking for some specifics here. What kind of plumbing fixtures do you have there? Like, I kind of assume that since you're mostly European, you probably have a bidet in the bathroom.

God: There is no plumbing in heaven. There are only harmonic waves of peace and abundance.

Me: Hmmm. Hard to wrap my brain around that. How many square feet is it?

God: It is the size of everything divided by infinity and then multiplied by endlessness.

Me: I have no idea what any of that means. What kind of wood kitchen cabinets do you have? I'm pegging you for fan of hickory. What are your countertops made from? Granite?

God: My countertops are made of truth.

Me: Huh. Okay...truth countertops...sure...

God: You don't understand any of this, do you?

Me: Not a word. Sometimes You can be a bit too mysterious.

God: This is probably why we talk about you all the time.

Me: Probably.

God: Hand me those toenail clippers. I'll help you out this time.

Me: Sweet! Thanks God!

God: By the way my kitchen cabinets are made of hickory.

Me: I knew it!

God: It's super classy.

Me: Can you believe how long my toenails are?

God: I can't. Maybe you are a mutant.
Me: My entire life makes sense now.

Autism?

Me: Hey God.

God: Hey John.

Me: Why did You create autism?

God: I didn't.

Me: Yes, You did.

God: I didn't create autism. I created people.

It's Really Just A Circle

Me: Hey God.

God: Hey John.

Me: I would like You to give me more money.

God: Okay. You should get a job to help with that.

Me: I'm not smart enough to get a job. I would like You to increase my IQ.

God: Alright. Perhaps you should read a book to increase your intelligence then.

Me: That sounds like work. I would like You to give me more determination to improve myself.

God: Gotcha. How about you hire a life coach to help with that then?

Me: That would be expensive. I would like You to give me more money.

God: Wow...

Me: It's a vicious circle.

Formalities

Me: I hail thee, oh God!

God: Um. Okay...hey John. Sorry I'm late. Were you waiting long?

Me: How lovely and righteously powerful Thou art!

God: Err. Thank you... How are things for you?

Me: The Heavens and Earth rejoice in Thy perfection!

God: Why are you talking like that?

Me: In Thane presence I approach with my sinful nature ready to surrender to You. My knees and voice quiver in lamentation.

God: That's enough.

Me: I marvel at all Your creation! You are the infallible potter and I am Your humble lump of unformed clay. I bend and I am shaped to Your artistic will!

God: Seriously. Stop it. Just be cool.

Me: How can I stop when I need to proclaim Your generosity to the edges of the universe?!!

God: Are you experiencing some sort of neurological event?

Me: In your honor I shall find the fattest calf and slaughter it on the peak of the highest hilltop.

God: I would actually back the fattest calf in that matchup. I have seen how hard you find it to put a child in a car seat.

Me: Please have mercy on me! I am not worthy to stand in the light of –

God: Knock it off!!

Me: Okay. I'm done now.

God: Good! Why were you doing that?

Me: I just wanted to pay my respects.

God: It felt a bit forced.

Me: Oh. Sorry.

God: Look, I appreciate the effort, but I still have no clue why you were talking like that.

Me: No real reason. I just wanted to try it out. I was hoping to brighten Your day.

God: Okay...that's nice. Confusing, but nice, I suppose.

Me: Can you lend me ten thousand dollars?

God: There we go. Now it all makes sense.

Me: Hear my cry oh glorious and supreme and beautiful and awesome God!

God: Oh boy…

Talking To Headstones

Me: Hey God.

God: Hey John.

Me: I have a question.

God: That's what I'm here for.

Me: I need a straight answer from You.

God: Sure!

Me: Just give me a "yes" or a "no", okay?

God: I'll give it a shot.

Me: Does grief ever go away?

God: Yes and no.

Me: That isn't a simple answer.

God: You asked a complicated question.

Me: I just want a "yes" or a "no".

God: I can't do that for you on this one.

Me: Since You can't answer I'm thinking that's Your way of saying that grief never goes away.

God: Uh, no, that isn't what I mean. Grief is tricky. It's like a unique puzzle for everyone. It's different from one person to the next.

Me: Great.

God: Is that why we are meeting at the cemetery?

Me: Yes. By the way, nice fog You brought in. Really adds to the ambiance.

God: Coincidence. Why are we talking about grief today?

Me: I'm tired of feeling like this. I'm tired of grief always sneaking under the door of my heart.

God: Is it your parents that you're grieving today?

Me: Yes. I don't know why.

God: I do.

Me: Enlighten me, please.

God: Words were left unsaid between you and them before they died.

Me: I never got to tell them how grateful I was.

God: They knew.

Me: I don't know that for sure.

God: Why don't you talk to them now?

Me: I don't want to be the cliché of the guy who sits in front of a headstone and rambles on. Besides, people might think I'm crazy.

God: I think that ship may have already sailed. You've been posting these conversations of ours for a few months now. I know for a fact that plenty of folks think you've lost your mind already.

Me: Are you saying that prayer is an act of insanity?

God: It is either an act of faith of a sign that you just enjoy talking to yourself.

Me: Which one is it?

God: Either one is possible with you.

Me: Again, not a real clear answer.

God: Having a spiritual life is a bit of a mystery, isn't it?

Me: My dad died when I was 23.

God: I know. I was there.

Me: He died before I got married. He died before my children were born. He hasn't seen the fruit of all his sacrifices and hard work.

God: He has.

Me: No offense, but I'd like to hear that from him.

God: I'm sure.

Me: Will you get him for me?

God: Things don't work like that.

Me: Why?

God: To uphold the mystery of this whole life experience. If everybody could chat with their deceased loved ones it would ruin everything I'm trying to cultivate here.

Me: Which is what?

God: That physical life is temporary and precious. Plus, it adds to the mystery of existence.

Me: Right. I hate mysteries.

God: You do? You used to love all the Hardy Boys books.

Me: Yeah, they were solving mysteries about missing mummies or dealing with Aztec curses. They didn't have to deduce the complex riddles of life.

God: True.

Me: I just needed an extra ten minutes with each of them.

God: Your parents know that you miss them. They know that you love them. Love doesn't go away. Not even in the afterlife. It's tangible. It's a real thing.

Me: Unconvinced.

God: Do you love your kids?

Me: Of course.

God: Are they here in front of you?

Me: No. They're at school.

God: Does that prevent you from loving them?

Me: No...

God: Same thing. The fact that you aren't physically together doesn't keep them from the love they feel towards you.

Me: I wish I had told them how I felt more often. Now I'm left with this grief and regret.

God: Those aren't necessarily bad things to feel.

Me: Why do you even allow these kinds of emotions?

God: Grief is a reminder that life is finite. There is a clock that is always ticking. There is only so much time to say everything you need to say or do the things you do. Once the buzzer sounds, that's it, you're done. Grief is telling you to live without regrets. To express your life and love right now because you never know when the curtain will drop for you.

Me: That is depressing.

God: It should make you feel the exact opposite. You should feel encouraged. Get your behind moving! Quit wasting time! Live your life! Don't miss any more opportunities! Haven't you allowed enough of your time to slip by? Seize the moment! Start today!

Me: How do I start, exactly?

God: By talking to these headstones. Don't fight the grief. Embrace it. Learn the lesson it's trying to teach you.

Me: Okay...

God: Tell your parents everything you wish you had while they were alive. Let them know that that you can still tap into the heartbreak you felt the day they passed. Or how lost you feel without them in your life. How you miss them helping rudder your ship. Spill your guts.

Me: Will they hear me?

God: Maybe.

Me: Ugh.

God: Mystery!!

ME: Hey God.

God: Hey John.

ME: Why didn't you make me perfect?

God: Because where would any of the fun be in that?

That'll Show 'Em

Me: Hey God.

God: Hey John.

Me: I'm ticked off.

God: Why?

Me: I have a passive aggressive neighbor. I hate it when people act like that!

God: That can be infuriating. You should talk to him about it.

Me: Nope. I have a better idea on how to get my message across.

God: What's that?

Me: I'm going to give him the silent treatment.

God: Um...

Alone

Me: Hey God.

God: Hey John.

Me: I spent 20 minutes alone in a church last night.

God: How was that experience for you?

Me: To be honest I found it very unsettling.

God: How so?

Me: It was just too quiet and still. Very eerie.

God: Why didn't you break the silence and talk to Me?

Me: You mean out loud?

God: Yeah.

Me: I find the thought of speaking to You out loud in an empty church absolutely terrifying.

God: Why? Are you scared that I may talk back to you?

Me: No... I'm scared that You won't.

Fear Sells!

Me: Hey God.

God: Hey John.

Me: The world is so violent.

God: Quit watching the news.

Me: People can be so evil to each other.

God: Quit watching the news.

Me: Things are getting worse every day.

God: Quit watching the news.

Me: I don't think there is any hope for us.

God: Quit watching the news.

Me: I can't.

God: Why?

Me: If I stop watching, how will I know what to be afraid of?

God: Exactly.

Me: Oh.

Plans

Me: Hey God.

God: Hey John.

Me: I'm excited.

God: How come?

Me: I'm writing out a new life plan.

God: Cool. However, just one thing...

Me: What?

God: Make sure you write it in pencil.

Me: Come on...

Secret Recipe

Me: Hey God

God: Hey John.

Me: What's the most important –

God: Unconditional love.

Me: What?

God: Weren't you trying to ask about what most important thing in life is?

Me: No, that's not what I was asking. I wanted to know what You thought was the most important ingredient to add if I wanted to make some amazing fried chicken.

God: My answer remains the same.

Missing Robin

Me: Hey God.

God: Hey John.

Me: It's been almost a year since Robin Williams took his own life.

God: It doesn't seem that long ago.

Me: I know. Normally celebrity deaths don't affect me like his did. It wasn't like I ever met him or anything, but even a year later, I'm still broken hearted about it.

God: Suicide is a horrible epidemic. Nobody is immune to it.

Me: Robin Williams was a genius...

God: He still is. We love him up here. He draws huge audiences.

Me: He was such an inspiration in my life.

God: He still can be. Death isn't the end of life. You know this.

Me: Tell Robin I miss him.

God: I will.

Me: It scares me to my core to know that somebody as talented as him can be lost to depression.

God: Hits too close to home, I bet.

Me: Sort of. Depression has always been the monster waiting under my bed. Waiting to pull me under with it.

God: It will only do that if you stop having hope.

Me: Hope? No matter how many obstacles I place in front of it or barriers that I build, depression always finds a way inside. Depression is like a ghost that can walk through walls. There is no escaping it. There is no hiding from it.

God: My advice is to quit hiding from it then.

Me: What does that mean?

God: Don't deny the existence of your depression. Stop trying to avoid it. Let it in. Let it have its moment with you and then let it leave.

Me: Will that keep it from coming back?

God: No. It will always come back. Depression is like a passing shadow that crawls across your floorboards. Yes, it will show up, but it will eventually give way to sunlight.

Me: That's a nice thought, but impossible to keep in mind when that shadow has completely enveloped me in its darkness.

God: Remember that shadows are temporary. Light is permanent. It's always there on the other side of darkness.

Me: I just wish depression would leave me alone. I don't understand why You even allow for it.

God: Without sadness and grief you would have no appreciation of joy and life. Without the darkness of night you would take the daylight for granted.

Me: I hope You are right about how the sunlight will always trump darkness.

God: I'm certain of it.

Me: How can You be?

God: Because I am the light. I'm glad that you finally talked to Me about this.

Me: I am too…

God: Shadows pass. Hope remains. I love you.

BA-DUM DA-DUM DA DA
DUM DUM!

Me: Hey God.

God: Hey John.

Me: On my way to an important meeting!

God: Alright!!

Me: I hope I don't screw it up.

God: You won't. Besides, I'll be there to help.

Me: What if there's a problem?

God: YO! I'LL SOLVE IT!!! CHECK OUT THE HOOK WHILE MY DJ REVOLVES IT!!

Me: Um...

God: BA-DUM DA-DUM DA DA DUM DUM!

Me:

God: Couldn't help it. You set Me up for some Vanilla Ice.

Me: Are You done?

God: WILL IT EVER STOP? YO I DON'T KNOW!! TURN OUT THE LIGHTS AND I'LL GLOW!

Me: Great. Now I have that song stuck in my head.

God: Yep.

JOHN ROEDEL

Me: I'm going to be late for my meeting. Let's get out of here.
God: WORD TO YOUR MOTHER!!

Imagine Better

Me: Hey God.

God: Hey John.

Me: Arrggh!

God: What's up?

Me: My dishwasher is leaking everywhere!

God: I thought you fixed it.

Me: I thought I did too but I think I made things worse. My wife isn't very happy with me.

God: I don't blame her. That's a lot of water.

Me: My whole day is ruined!

God: Over a broken dishwasher? Aren't you going to call someone to come and fix it?

Me: Yes, but they will probably be super expensive and knowing my luck they won't be able to fix the problem. So, my dishwasher will keep leaking until my entire kitchen is ruined. Eventually the damage will be so horrible that my home will collapse into a big pile of mud and unfinished laundry. Then the reporters will show up and run a story about how I ruined my family's life by trying to fix the dishwasher myself. Which means that we will all have to move into the woods and live amongst the poison ivy and brambles. Then the local bear will show up to challenge me to a fight to see who gets to be king of the forest. And of course I'll lose to the bear and end up at the bottom of his stomach. Within two weeks of my demise there will be a really unflattering SNL sketch about my tragic death and my children will have to change their last names in order to have a chance at being accepted into college someday.

God: Wow...your anxiety is high today.

Me: I know.

God: You think all of that will happen because your dishwasher is leaking?

Me: I'm pretty sure of it.

God: Your life would be so much easier if you maintained a more positive outlook whenever problems come your way.

Me: Maybe.

God: What do you suppose the best-case scenario for your broken dishwasher is?

Me: That I'll call somebody and they will come and fix it. Then I'll go get a couple of tacos to celebrate.

God: That sounds nice. Why don't you picture that happening instead all of those horrible things you are imagining?

Me: Yeah, good point. Let's go with that option. I'd rather not be eaten by a bear.

God: The only bear in your life is your anxiety. Quit feeding it.

Me: How?

God: By using your imagination for good. I didn't give you the power of creativity to torture yourself with it. Let your imagination have a chance to paint a future that you will love.

Me: I'll try. I promise. I'll try.

God: Great! Because I have some bad news for you.

Me: What?

God: Your microwave just caught fire.

Peace Prayer

Me: Hey God.

God: Hey John.

Me: I can't take the violence that exists down here anymore.

God: Good.

Me: How is that good?

God: Maybe you'll finally do something about it.

Me: That's your job.

God: I'm not an interventionist kind of God these days.

Me: I wish you were. It'd make things easier.

God: It's up to you to push back against fear and violence.

Me: How?

God: Commit this to memory:

> *Lord, make me an instrument of your peace,*
> *Where there is hatred, let me sow love;*
> *where there is injury, pardon;*
> *where there is doubt, faith;*
> *where there is despair, hope;*
> *where there is darkness, light;*

where there is sadness, joy.

Me: Isn't that a part of The Prayer Of Saint Francis?

God: Yes. I love it. Make it a part of your day today.

Me: I'm scared of the world I live in.

God: Don't be. It's beautiful. Help reflect that beauty. Combat violence with kindness and hope.

Me: I'll try. How do I start?

God: By turning off the news.

Me: Um...no. How will I know about all the horrible things that are happening around the world?

God: You won't. Those things will exist with or without your knowledge of them. Quit giving fear power over your life.

Me: So, I quit obsessing over terrible news stories? Then what?

God: Then? Then you go out and get to work.

Me: I'd rather stay at home with my dogs. It's safer.

God: That's exactly what Saint Francis said.

Job Market

Me: Hey God.

God: Hey John.

Me: I'm updating my résumé.

God: Really??

Me: Yep. I found a job that is perfect for my skill set.

God: Wow. That's a huge step towards actually doing something with your life.

Me: Thanks! I figured it's time to get back into the workforce. The world needs me. I'm like Batman.

God: You're more like the Penguin.

Me: Would You mind if I put You down as a reference?

God: Sure.

Me: Just make sure that whenever somebody calls You to check in on me that You tell them how amazing and attractive I am.

God: I'll give them a full report of all of your strengths and weaknesses.

Me: Stay away from my weaknesses. Focus more on the things that make me sound like a stud.

God: What would you like Me to say?

Me: You could tell them what a good people person I am.

God: You're terrible with people.

Me: I'm not that bad.

God: Your people skills are right above that of an acorn and just below that of a TSA agent.

Me: You should also tell whoever is calling how adept I am at crunching numbers and managing finances.

God: Errrr...you frequently lose your wallet and have never ever balanced your checkbook.

Me: I balanced it last month!

God: That's because you ran out of money! It kind of balances itself when that happens! You have no idea how to manage money.

Me: That's because math is hard.

God: Use a calculator then.

Me: Calculators are tricky.

God: Have your nine-year-old son show you how to use it.

Me: Then You should let my potential employer know that I'm a team player who is also a serious go-getter.

God: So, I should stay away from the fact that you hate working with others and that you are allergic to actual work?

Me: Definitely don't mention any of that.

God: Or how you require seven naps per day?

Me: That is none of their business anyway.

God: Look, John, I'm not going to lie for you.

Me: Don't screw this up for me!

God: I'll just tell them about the greatest attribute that I've given you. That's all I can do.

Me: Which attribute is that?

God: You have really nice hair.

Me: Perfect!

God: It is? What job are you applying for?

Me: Game Show Host.

God: Nice.

Art!

Me: Hey God.

God: Hey John.

Me: I feel broken.

God: That's because you are broken. You've been this way a very long time.

Me: I feel like a glass that shattered all over the floor. There are a thousand little pieces of me scattered everywhere.

God: Are you asking Me to put you back together again?

Me: Not the way I was. Make me into something new.

God: Any requests?

Me: Turn my broken pieces into art.

God: I'm on it.

Here They Come!

Me: Hey God.

God: Hey John.

Me: I'm ready to start the day. Let's go Out There!

God: Super! There's the front door.

Me: There it is.

God: Let's go.

Me: You bet.

God: Uh, you're not moving.

Me: I'm not?

God: No.

Me: How about now?

God: You're just standing there.

Me: Alright. I'm ready now. Here we go!

God: Here we go! The day awaits!

Me: I'm still not moving, am I?

God: Nope. What's up?

Me: I think I'm too scared to go Out There today. Out There is scary and chaotic. I'll try again tomorrow. In Here is safe and comfortable. Out There is a mess. In Here is neat and tidy. I know where everything is In Here. I know what's going to happen to me In Here. Out There is a frightening jungle of uncontrollable things and people.

God: It's an adventure Out There! Go have one!

Me: Maybe later...

God: I didn't make you to hide away like this. I didn't make you for In Here. I made you to be Out There in the mix of life. I know it's a bit crazy and wild Out There, but that is kind of the point. In Here is way overrated.

Me: Right.

God: Try again?

Me: You bet. I'm ready to go!

God: There's the front door.

Me: There it is...

God: You're still not moving.

Me: It's not going to happen.

God: Why?

Me: I just don't think I can fake it out there today.

God: Fake what?

Me: Fake being happy.

God: Why would you do that?

Me: Because that's what we are supposed do out there. I smile and say everything is great and wonderful even when it's not, which has been the case for a long time. Fake happiness is really a hard act to keep going.

God: Don't do it then. If you are in pain, let people know. Don't suffer alone In Here.

Me: Well, I have found that I don't get invited to many parties because when people ask me how I am and I respond with "I'm doing fine...except for this dark sludge that I feel in my heart that is trying to eat its way through my chest cavity. And how are you?" it can get awkward. So, I just answer with "I'm doing great!" with the best Oscar winning performance I can muster. I just fake it out there until I'm safe and sound back In Here.

God: But if you don't tell anyone that you are suffering, there is no way for them to know that you need help. There is no shame in asking other people for help. Everybody needs it at some point in their life. Everybody can get broken. People need each other. That's one of the best things about leaving In Here and going Out There, you all can listen to and heal each other. You are never supposed to fake it. You are supposed to be honest and lean on each other when you need to. Quit closing yourself off from others and start relying on other people.

Me: People can be hurtful.

God: They can also be wonderful. Ask them for help. Just call out and they'll come running.

Me: In Here nothing bad happens to me.

God: Correction: In Here nothing happens to you at all. This isn't living. It's just waiting. Get out there. If you are hurting, find somebody who will help you. Don't suffer alone. Then you can turn around and help somebody else who is in pain.

Me: How can I tell if somebody else is in pain?

God: Fake smiles are easy to pick out.

Me: They are?

God: Yeah, you're not really fooling anybody. Just be on the lookout for people who are desperate to go back to their own personal "In Here."

Me: That's not very grammatically correct.

God: I'm allowed.

Me: Alright. Let's try this again. I'm ready to start the day. Let's go Out There!

God: Super! Get going.

Me: Hand on the doorknob...

God: Just turn the handle. Let's go ask for some help.

Me: Whoa. So bright.

God: I love it Out There...

Me: Hello, I need help....

God: Here they come!

Nothing To Cure

Me: Hey God.

God: Hey John.

Me: Cure autism.

God: No.

Me: Why?

God: There is nothing to cure.

Me: Huh?

God: Autistic people aren't broken. They aren't sick. They are just people singing a beautiful song with lyrics that are foreign to you.

Me: But sometimes I don't understand what song my son is singing...

God: That's okay. Forget the lyrics and just sit back and enjoy the melody.

Me: I don't like to see him struggle.

God: All flowers struggle just before they blossom.

Me: If you won't cure autism, what will you do?

God: I'll have you help me cure something else.

Me: What's that?

God: Ignorance.

Nonetheless

Me: Hey God.

God: Hey John.

Me: Do You love me?

God: Yes.

Me: Unconditionally?

God: Yes.

Me: Why?

God: Because I made you.

Me: That doesn't seem like a good enough reason for unconditional love. I make horrible mistakes daily.

God: Just like everybody else. And just like everybody else I will continue to love you nonetheless.

Me: Nonetheless?

God: Nonetheless.

Me: I love that word.

God: Me too.

Me: You love us because You made us? It's really that simple?

God: Right.

Me: But we are all such a hot toxic rabbit dung fire here on Earth.

God: I wouldn't say that. I like to think that everybody I create is simply a perpetual work in progress.

Me: That has to be really frustrating for You.

God: Not really. Each of you is like an early draft of a unique poem. A little rough, but full of potential for great beauty and meaning.

Me: So, our lives are all like a poem?

God: Yes.

Me: I really like that thought. Even me? You consider my life a form of poetry?

God: Well, yours is more like a dirty bathroom limerick.

Me: But a poem nonetheless?

God: Nonetheless!

Me: I love that word.

God: And I love you. Nonetheless.

Sigh

Me: Hey God.

God: Hey John.

Me: Sigh.

God: What's wrong?

Me: Nothing... Sigh!

God: Seriously...what's up? You're huffing and puffing all over everybody.

Me: I'm just tired of people gossiping about me all the time.

God: Um, what are you talking about?

Me: Being the constant topic of other people's conversation is simply exhausting for me.

God: Nobody is gossiping about you. I can't remember the last time somebody mentioned your name when you weren't around. You absolutely don't have to worry about people talking about you.

Me: SIGH!!!

God: What's wrong now?

Me: I'm tired of people ignoring me all the time.

God: Of course you are.

Accountability

Me: Hey God.

God: Hey John.

Me: Who have I become?

God: You're the sum of all the choices that you have made in your life.

Me: What does that mean?

God: It means that you have become the person that you have chosen to be.

Me: Shoot. That doesn't really offer me much room to blame other people for my problems or character defects.

God: Not really, no.

Me: Is there anything I can do to escape all accountability for decisions that I make?

God: Yes. There is one thing you can do.

Me: What is it?

God: Get elected to Congress.

Me: Ha! Nice one!

God: I'm not kidding.

It's The Other Way Around

Me: Hey God.

God: Hey John.

Me: I feel paralyzed.

God: Why?

Me: Depression has a tight grip on me today.

God: No, it doesn't.

Me: Then why can't I move out of bed?

God: Depression.

Me: See! I told you that depression is holding on to me.

God: Nope. It's the other way around.

Me: What does that mean?

God: You're the one holding on to depression.

Me: I am?

God: Time to let it go.

Me: Then what happens?

God: Everything.

Different IS Beautiful

Me: Hey God.

God: Hey John.

Me: I'm worried about my autistic son.

God: Why?

Me: I just want him to fit in with everybody else.

God: Don't ever say that again.

Me: What? Why?

God: Conformity is one of the worst things a parent could ever wish for their child.

Me: Oops.

God: Remember what yours has taught you.

Me: Different is NOT broken.

God: Different IS beautiful.

Me: Thanks for the reminder.

God: I'm not the one reminding you.

The Creative Process

Me: Hey God.

God: Hey John.

Me: Was it hard to create everything?

God: Not at all.

Me: Really?

God: Creation is the easy part.

Me: What's the hard part?

God: Knowing that people hardly ever take any notice of it.

Me: That's not fair.

God: When was the last time you just stared at a single flower in a garden to reflect on how much design and care I put into it simply for it to exist?

Me: Uh, never. Flowers scare me.

God: Wasps?

Me: Wasps. They are nature's sociopathic hit man.

God: Have you ever thought about the wonders of all the subatomic particles that exist all around you?

Me: Not even once.

God: Do you ever stop and consider how vast the Universe is? There is an infinite web of galaxies spiraling out there beyond your atmosphere that you never ever think about.

Me: I have watched every single episode of Battlestar Galactica if that helps.

God: It doesn't. I just wish you'd spend a little more time in awe and wonderment of everything that I've made. It is a masterpiece and I'm bummed that you take it for granted.

Me: Wow. You're kind of grumpy tonight.

God: You would be too if your divine artistry wasn't being appreciated.

Me: Hold on, let me get my passport.

God: What do you need a passport for?

Me: Because You're taking me on a huge guilt trip.

God: Nice.

Me: I'm sorry I'm ungrateful for everything You've made. I'll stop taking creation for granted.

God: That would be great!

Me: Except for wasps. They're real jerks.

God: You'll get no argument from Me.

Don't Mean Nothing!

Me: Hey God.

God: Hey John.

Me: I've been trying to talk to You. Where have You been?

God: Right here waiting for you.

Me: Well, I'm having a hard time with my faith life lately. I'm having doubts. Can you tell me what that means?

God: Don't mean nothing.

Me: Huh? That's a double negative. Anyway, last night I couldn't sleep because I was wondering if You were real or not.

God: You should have known better.

Me: I know. But my doubts are always at their worst when I'm trying to go to sleep. What should I do?

God: Hold onto the nights.

Me: What?

God: Satisfied?

Me: No! I am having a hard time understanding You today.

God: One more try.

Me: Fine. I'll ask You again. What should I do about my lack of faith and why I haven't been talking to You lately?

God: Keep coming back.

Me: I do but – wait a second, are You just saying the names of Richard Marx songs? Is that what You are doing?

God: Nothing to hide.

Me: I'll take that as a "yes". This is frustrating. Will You please stop?

God: Endless summer nights.

Me: That answer doesn't even work.

God: Take it to heart?

Me: That doesn't work either.

God: You're right. I ran out of good songs to use. I was just having some fun.

Me: Whatever.

God: Don't worry so much about your doubts in Me. Remember doubt is good. It keeps you curious and asking questions. I like questions.

Me: But sometimes I worry if You care about me.

God: I do.

Me: You do?

God: Now and forever.

Me: Is that just a Richard Marx song title or is that Your real answer?

God: Both.

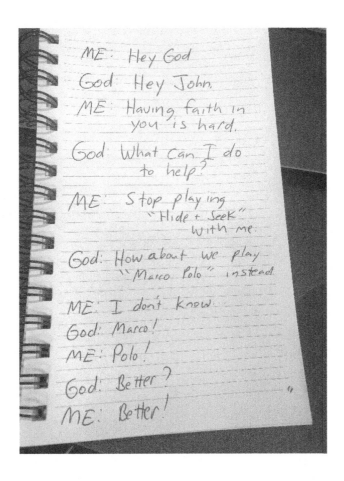

Faith Crisis

Me: Hey God.

God: Hey John.

Me: Thanks for being so patient with my faith crisis.

God: Sure, but I think it's been going on too long now to be classified as a "crisis".

Me: How long have I been doubting You?

God: About a decade now. A crisis usually only lasts a short while.

Me: Like when Hostess said they weren't going to make any more Twinkies or Ding Dongs?

God: Um. I guess. I was thinking about more serious –

Me: Those were dark days. I gained some stress weight during that horrible time.

God: I think you were the only person who gained body fat during a processed baked goods shortage.

Me: I wasn't sure if I wanted to live in a world without vacuum-sealed pastries that can outlast a nuclear winter.

God: Don't worry. If you're alive there will always be a Ding Dong on Earth.

Me: Ouch!

God: Heh.

Me: So, if You don't think I'm having a faith crisis, what do You think has been going on with me?

God: You doubt. It's that simple. It's not an evolving situation. It's who you are right now.

Me: When will it pass?

God: That's pretty much up to you. I can't make you believe in Me. That's why it's called faith.

Me: I do believe in You.

God: You do?

Me: Yeah. On Sundays.

God: Right. That means that you believe in Me a seventh of the time. That's not a very good average.

Me: Make it easier to believe in You, then!

God: I did. You are surrounded by miracles.

Me: Where?

God: Look around you. It's all a miracle. It's all a gift. There used to be nothing here. Nothing. Now there is creation everywhere. Each breath that you mindlessly inhale is an act of creation. Life is all around you. It's all a gift, but you ignore it because it's easier not to believe in Me. I've made all of this. From the countless stars and expanding Universe above you, to the blades of grass and grains of sand beneath you. The people in your life. I put them there. It's all a gift. It's all a miracle. It's all My love letter to you.

Me: Huh.

God: Was that a little too much for you to think about?

Me: Probably.

God: I take it that you are still having doubts in Me?

Me: Yeah. Sorry. I really am.

God: I know. Don't worry about it. I'll be here when you finally get it.

Me: Thanks. You are so patient.

God: I have all the time in the world.

Me: You sure do.

God: But you don't, Ding Dong

Step One

Me: Hey God.

God: Hey John.

Me: I hate being jealous of other people.

God: I have an amazing step-by-step plan on how you can stop envying other people. Want to hear it?

Me: Sure do!

God: Make sure you write it down so you won't forget it.

Me: Okay, go ahead.

God: Step One: Be grateful for what you already have.

Me: Got it.

God: Great.

Me: What's the second step?

God: There is no second step.

Act II:
Hey God, this is
getting a bit weird.

Every morning I wake up
and instantly begin to worry
about what I am going to type
to God.
I'm starting to dig into subjects that I have never
thought about before. I am starting to uncover
parts of me that haven't seen the sun in years.
What will people think about me?
What will I think about myself?
What will God think of me?
Every morning I want to quit and say goodbye to
these conversations.
I keep showing up.
God is always there waiting.
"Something is happening here.
What it is ain't exactly clear."

—Buffalo Springfield

Hands

Me: Hey God.

God: Hey John.

Me: My hands won't stop shaking.

God: I'm here. I'm right here.

Me: I think I'm having a panic attack.

God: What do you think is causing it?

Me: There are a hundred million reasons. It's not one thing, it's everything. It's like I'm being crushed by the weight of everything in my life. I'm sure that doesn't make much sense to You.

God: It does.

Me: I just need You to tell me that everything is going to be okay.

God: Everything is going to be more than okay. Everything is going to be awesome! Everything is going to wrap you up in its arms and hold you until your hands stop shaking. Everything is going to love you more than you can possibly ever measure.

Me: How can you possibly know that?

God: Because I am everything.

Me: Please help me.

God: Give me your hands and I'll take care of everything.

All These Things I've Done

Me: Hey God.

God: Hey John.

Me: I can't get my life going. It feels like I'm trapped in a small room with all the mistakes that I've made in my past.

God: Go through the door.

Me: There is no door. I'm stuck in here.

God: Let's build a door then. It won't be so hard.

Me: How?

God: By being forgiven.

Me: That won't work. I have asked and You have forgiven me ten thousand times and I'm still locked up in here.

God: That is because you're supposed to ask somebody else for forgiveness too.

Me: Who?

God: Yourself.

Me: Oh...

God: There isn't a way out of that room until you forgive yourself. If you want to leave through a door, you need to place your hands on your heart and truly forgive yourself.

Me: It's not that simple. I have made a lot of bad choices.

God: I know and it's time for you to leave all your mistakes and get out of there so you can go live your life.

Me: I forgive myself. There I said it. I still don't see a door.

God: That's because you didn't mean it. Say it again.

Me: I forgive myself.

God: Again.

Me: I forgive myself.

God: Like you mean it.

Me: I forgive myself!!

God: Nice.

Me: I don't see a door yet...

God: You need to believe that you are forgiven. Write "I forgive myself" on a piece of paper and carry it with you in your pocket. Write it on your wrist. Write it on your walls. Write it everywhere. Write "I forgive myself" over and over until the way out appears. Once out of there you will finally get to see what I have planned for you.

Me: What's that?

God: A big, fat, beautiful life.

Me: That's exactly what I want!

God: You know what to do then...

Me: I forgive myself. I forgive myself. I forgive myself. I forgive myself.

God: Keep going!

Me: I forgive myself! I forgive myself!

God: I think I see the corners of the door forming. You're almost ready. Say it again!

Me:

New Eyes

Me: Hey God.

God: Hey John.

God: Why are you sitting in there all alone in the dark?

Me: I'm hiding so that nothing can hurt me again.

God: The dark won't prevent you from being hurt. You can still be wounded in there, you just won't see it coming. Come out. The light is waiting.

Me: No. I told you, I don't want to. I'm afraid of being hurt in the light.

God: Stop fibbing. You aren't afraid of being hurt out here.

Me: What am I afraid of then?

God: Being healed. Wounds will never heal until you let them. Scars will never form until you look at them in the light. You'll never be able to forgive yourself in there, in the dark. Forgiveness and healing are fruits of the light. Come out. Come out. It's time. I love you, come out.

Me: I don't think I can. I've gotten too used to it in here.

God: Yes, you can. I'll give you new eyes to help you out.

Me: With what? The brightness?

God: No, the eyes are so that you can finally see yourself the way that I see you:

Beautiful. Worthy. Brave. Forgiven. Come out. Come out. I love you. Come out.

Your Past Has No Fingers

Me: Hey God.

God: Hey John.

Me: My past is holding me down.

God: That's impossible.

Me: Why? I feel tied to it.

God: Your past doesn't have any fingers. It can't tie anything. You're the one who has knotted yourself to its wrist.

Me: I've made too many mistakes ever to be free of it.

God: Forgiveness begins with the simple act of untying yourself from who you used to be. So you can be free to fly away and become something new and beautiful.

Me: Here I go...

Guilt: Bye John.

Me: I'm floating!

God: Enjoy the view!

Pieces

Me: Hey God.

God: Hey John.

Me: It's not even lunch and I've already fallen to pieces.

God: That's totally fine. I like pieces. It makes you look like a mosaic.

Me: I just wish my life were more put together.

God: I don't.

Me: Why not?

God: Because I like puzzles. I can help you if you'd like?

Me: That would be great. Here is the cover of my puzzle box. We can use the picture as a guide to show us how my life is supposed to look like.

God: Oh, we won't need it. Your puzzle isn't ever going to look anything like that picture.

Me: Really? The guy looks so happy, plus he has zero evidence of a unibrow.

God: Sorry. Your life doesn't have the puzzle pieces to make a picture like that.

Me: Aw.

God: Yep.

Me: Fine. What's next? Should we first find all of the straight edges of my puzzle so we can build its frame?

God: We are going to throw out all the edges and border pieces. You won't need them.

Me: How will we know where my boundaries are?

God: You don't have any. Your life has infinite possibilities.

Me: I don't understand. Without any boundaries I won't know which way to build.

God: Exactly.

Me: What? How do I know when I'm done putting myself together?

God: There is no "done" because your puzzle won't ever be finished.

Me: That's discouraging.

God: I think it's exciting!

Me: I wanted my life to look like the guy on the cover of the puzzle box. That is how it's supposed to look.

God: Nobody's looks like that. Everybody is constantly shuffling their pieces together.

Nobody is ever finished. It's the joyful work of a lifetime.

Me: Wait. My pieces won't even fit together? There are hardly any matches. How am I going to get this thing to stay together with all these jagged pieces?

God: That's where I come in. I'm the glue.

Me: This is going to get messy.

God: I can't wait! Let's get started.

Me: We are going to need a bigger table.

Mother's Day In Heaven

Me: Hey God.

God: Hey John.

Me: Do You celebrate Mother's Day in heaven?

God: Every day is Mother's Day in heaven.

Me: Nice. Can you tell my mom that I miss her?

God: I just did.

Me: Did she have a message for me?

God: Yeah, your mom says that you need to cut your hair, quit wasting your money on brand name groceries and to try eating with a fork sometime.

Me: Wow. It's like she never left.

God: That's because she never did.

Needs

Me: Hey God.

God: Hey John.

Me: I need –

God: No, you don't.

Me: You didn't let me finish.

God: Didn't have to. Whenever you start a sentence with "I need" it always ends with something ridiculous.

Me: Not always.

God: Always. Yesterday you told Me that you "needed" Me to help you find a waffle that was shaped like Ted Cruz.

Me: It was for a YouTube video I'm working on. It's called "Waffle Caucus". I already have all the other candidates lined up. I discovered a frozen Ego Waffle in the back of my freezer that looks like a happy Bernie Sanders.

God: That's weird. And just before that request you asked Me to help you communicate with the rabbits because you "needed" to reason with them.

Me: They are getting it on every night in the planter right under my bedroom window! I can't sleep with all that bunny love going on!

God: Then a couple hours ago you said that you "needed" somebody selling jelly-filled donuts door-to-door to show up at your house.

Me: I'm still waiting for that person to show up by the way. Tell them to just come on in the house. If I'm asleep on the couch, they can feed me while I'm unconscious.

God: Nobody is coming.

Me: Aw.

God: I don't know what is worse: The fact that you only live two blocks away from a place that sells donuts and yet you are too lazy to walk over there and get them. Or that you would be willing to buy baked goods from a random stranger who showed up at your door.

Me: I think it's a tie.

God: You should quit using the words "I need" before you ask Me for things. Words matter. You are constantly choosing words that make it sound like you have nothing, when the truth is you have so much.

Me: So, I should be saying "I want" instead? That seems greedy.

God: At least it would be more honest. You don't need most of these things. You want them. The word "need" is a sacred word that should only be used for things that really matter and are essential to life.

Me: Gotcha.

God: This whole want versus need story is a serious pet peeve of Mine.

Me: I bet. Can we start over this morning?

God: That would be great!

Me: Hey God.

God: Hey John.

Me: I need You to help me to –

God: John! That is exactly the thing you shouldn't –

Me: ...be more grateful for everything I already have.

God: Nice!

It Always Comes Back

Me: Hey God.

God: Hey John.

Me: I'm tired of feeling sad.

God: That's because you're resisting it. You keep sadness alive by fighting so hard against it all the time.

Me: Shouldn't I be?

God: Nope. Embrace it. Let the sadness have its moment with you. Let it go and move on to whatever is coming next. Darkness can get sticky if you let it linger anywhere near your heart. Don't deny it exists. Examine where it is coming from. Look for the source of your sadness. Put a light on it. Then just let it pass through you. Quit holding on to it.

Me: I'm scared that it will come back.

God: It will. Depression is like a river that is in a constant state of ebb and flow. One day the water will be slow and the next it will be full of whitewater currents. You just need to find a way to navigate it every day without being swept away.

Me: I don't think I can. Eventually this river is going to swallow me up.

God: Don't worry. I'll be your bridge across the river whenever you need Me.

Me: I wish depression would just go away.

God: It won't. It waxes and wanes like the moon. But pay it no mind because I'll forever remain your bridge. Let go of your need to fight the river alone. Give Me your hand. Let's cross this sucker together.

Stuck

Me: Hey God.

God: Hey John.

Me: I'm stuck.

God: I'd say.

Me: Can you help me?

God: First of all, it's time to admit to yourself that those skinny jeans are not ideal for your current body shape.

Me: Wait –

God: Here is some free advice:

Untie the constraints of whatever no longer fits your life. Quit trying to wear the clothes of someone that you're not. You've jammed yourself into something that makes you feel trapped, but you're not. Get out of it now. Allow for some room and the flexibility to dance at a moment's notice. Right now you look super uncomfortable and it's time for you to release what you perceive others people expect of you. You were born to feel free, not constricted. Life is too short to spend it suffering. Change, John, change. I can't do it for you. You must do it yourself.

Me: God, I'm not talking about my pants. I'm talking about my life. I feel stuck.

God: I'm talking about your pants AND your life!

Me: I can't breathe.

God: I bet. My divine wisdom can help you to do that.

Me: No, now it's the pants. They are way too tight and I can't feel my thighs.

God: Let's find your wife and a pair of scissors so she can cut you out of them.

Insomnia

Me: Hey God.

God: Hey John.

Me: My insomnia is getting worse.

God: I noticed.

Me: I just can't turn off my brain.

God: It's all your constant worrying that keeps your mind racing.

Me: I have about ten thousand things that I'm worrying about at any given time.

God: I know. You need to get rid of the worries that you can't control.

Me: I'll try, but what will I do with all the other remaining worries?

God: There will only be one worry left that you have any power over.

Me: Which one is that?

God: How fearlessly you will love.

Know Doubt

Me: Hey God.

God: Hey John.

Me: I have doubts.

God: Great! Keep at it!

Me: That's not a good thing.

God: It's a sign that you're still exploring and struggling with your faith. It means that you're still at work. I'll take it!

Me: Why do you allow me to doubt in You?

God: Because I gave you free will. I don't want zombie believers.

Me: I'm tired of doubting. Get rid of it.

God: You want no doubt?

Me: Exactly.

God: Nope. I want you to know doubt.

Me: Huh?

God: Come to understand your doubts. Where are they coming from? What are they telling you?

Me: I just wish it were easier to have faith. It shouldn't be this much work. I'm exhausted.

God: It should be work. Explore! Doubt! Struggle! Ask questions! Yell! Scream! It's all part of your journey to find Me.

Me: When will I stop doubting? It's exhausting...

God: Someday you'll realize that having doubt takes a lot more work and effort than having faith.

Me: Then what?

God: Then on that day you can rest in Me.

Me: I hope that day comes soon.

God: No doubt...

Me: Know doubt.

God: That's better.

On Joy

Me: Hey God.

God: Hey John.

Me: I'm ready to stop taking things so seriously.

God: Great!

Me: How do I start to do that?

God: First you must make a commitment to leading a joyful life.

Me: A joyful life?

God: Yeah, pursue joy always. Keep looking for it, even amid suffering. Choose joy every day. The world will tell you to surrender to guilt, pain, grudges, whatever, but ignore that. Surrender to joy. Choose joy. Choose joy. Choose joy!

Me: That sounds like a lot of work.

God: It will be at first, but with some practice it will become second nature to you. Choose joy!

Me: Ugh. Fine. I'll choose joy. But don't expect me to be happy about it...

God: Um...maybe I'm not explaining this right...

Windows And Doors

Me: Hey God.

God: Hey John.

Me: Can't talk today. I'm too depressed.

God: That's fine. I can just sit here with you.

Me: Alright.

God: Can I get you anything?

Me: Chocolate Haagen-Dazs ice cream.

God: Sure. How much?

Me: I want all the Chocolate Haagen-Dazs ice cream in the world.

God: That doesn't seem like a good idea. How about a glass of water?

Me: Chocolate water?

God: That's not a real thing.

Me: It should be.

God: What does your depression feel like?

Me: It feels different every day. Today I feel like I'm trapped in an abandoned house without windows or doors. I can hear what's going on outside, but there is no way of seeing it. I just sit by the walls and listen to the birds and the people walking by.

God: Being trapped inside yourself sounds really lonely.

Me: It is. I'm surrounded by life but I'm not a part of it.

God: This feeling will pass. It always does.

Me: I know. I just don't think I'll be very good company for a while.

God: There is so much beauty out there in the world. Eventually you won't be able to resist.

Me: Resist what?

God: Getting your butt out of bed and helping me make a couple of windows, so you can be reminded of what is waiting for you on the other side of depression.

Me: Why don't we just make a door?

God: First windows, then doors. Let's take it one step at a time.

Me: Can they at least be chocolate windows?

Word For Word

Me: Hey God.

God: Hey John.

Me: I can't sleep. Because I'm really frustrated with You!!!

God: Whoa. What did I do?

Me: It's more about what You're NOT doing!

God: Okay, let me have it.

Me: You allow way too much suffering on Earth. People need You to help them! They need You to not be so absent to the pain that exists in the world! Your hands-off approach isn't working! It's time for You to jump into the fray and help people not to feel so alone. People want to witness and feel Your love for them! Come on! What are You waiting for?

God: Huh. That's funny.

Me: How is any of that funny?!

God: Because I was just about to say those exact same things to you.

Me: You were?

God: Word for word. Crazy, huh?

Parenthood

Me: Hey God.

God: Hey John.

Me: Being a parent is super stressful.

God: It kind of comes with the job.

Me: I wish my kids appreciated how much I worry and fret about them.

God: How do you express those concerns for them?

Me: By yelling at them about stupid things.

God: Uh huh...

Me: But only because I love them.

God: And you demonstrate that love to them through yelling?

Me: Correct.

God: You know how crazy that sounds, right?

Me: I'm like a beloved drill sergeant from an old war movie.

God: Uh, you're more like a crazy dude who always smells like ranch dressing and flips out at his children over leaving their underwear all over the floor.

Me: I just want my kids to be happy and responsible people.

God: You can't yell somebody into being happy.

Me: What do You suggest I do?

God: If you want your kids to lead a happy and purposeful life, show them one. Give them a model they can follow. Lead by example.

Me: Then what?

God: Then ease up on the micromanaging and the yelling and learn that there are times in which you need to get out of their way. Let them make mistakes. Let your kids fail. Then help them back up. Forgive and love them unconditionally.

Me: Sounds familiar.

God: I'm leading by example.

Simple Request

Me: Hey God.

God: Hey John.

Me: I have one simple request today.

God: Go for it.

Me: I would like my life to be perfect.

God: Nope.

Me: Why not?

God: Because where would the fun be in that?

Me: Okay...can You at least help me make my life a little bit easier?

God: Sure. It's a pretty simple trick, actually. You just need to stop blaming yourself for things that aren't your fault.

Me: I don't do that...do I?

God: Every day. Every time you do that you are just borrowing more needless suffering to bear. Not everything bad that's happened to you is because of something you did.

Me: Yeah but –

God: Hush. Sometimes bad things will happen to you and it won't be because you did something wrong. You keep punishing yourself for events or problems that are beyond your control. You put yourself in an emotional prison for crimes that you did not commit.

Me: Sometimes it's easier to just take the blame myself.

God: And sometimes nobody is to blame. You live in a world of extreme finger-pointing where everybody is obsessed with finding out who is to blame when things go bad, and you like to take a lot of that on your shoulders. If you want your life to be a little easier, quit punishing yourself with self-inflicted wounds.

Me: You are forgetting that I make a lot of mistakes.

God: Oh, I know you do. You make a ton of mistakes. Like, seriously, a ton of mistakes.

Me: Point taken...

God: I'm not talking about those mistakes. I'm talking about all of the times you blame yourself for mistakes or situations that are clearly not your fault. In fact, in the last week you have only been responsible for 23% of the hundreds of situations where you have blamed yourself or offered an apology. I didn't create you to have you spend your whole life apologizing.

Me: You're right. Sorry about that.

God: John...

Me: I'm joking!

God: I'm not. Stop burdening yourself with senseless guilt.

Me: How?

God: Grab a small slip of paper and write something down that you should have told yourself years ago...

Me: What's that?

God: I think you know.

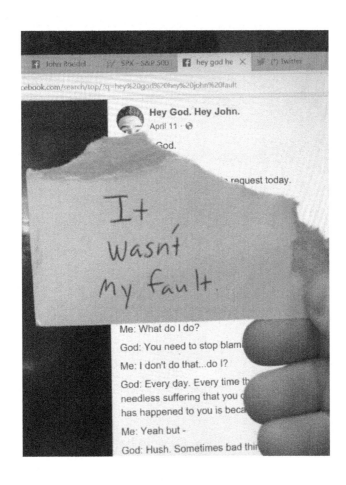

The Way

Me: Hey God.

God: Hey John.

Me: Show me the way.

God: I did.

Me: Show me the way again, please.

God: I did.

Me: Hmmm. Can You show me the way right now?

God: I am.

Me: Maybe You should just go ahead and play it on a loop until I see it?

God: Good idea.

Practice

Me: Hey God.

God: Hey John.

Me: I give up.

God: You can't.

Me: Why not?

God: Because I have a job for you. I need you to give a quick smile at a stranger later today.

Me: How come?

God: Because they are giving up, just like you are. But don't worry – I've spoken to this person already and they have agreed to smile back at you.

Me: And just what do You think You'll accomplish by having two hurt people smile at each other?

God: A flash will occur between the two of you.

Me: A flash of what?

God: Hope. Connection. Empathy. Understanding. Compassion. Community. Healing. Reassurance. Support. Empowerment. Kindness. Concern. Mercy. Faith. Goodwill.

Humanity.   Optimism.   Renewal.   Courage.
Decency. Generosity.

Me: I don't think I am able to produce a smile that can do all of that.

God: Then you better start practicing.

Touch The Sun

Me: Hey God.

God: Hey John.

Me: I hate feeling so depressed on such a sunny day.

God: I know.

Me: I feel so far removed from the sunlight. I can see it on my skin but I can't feel any of its warmth.

God: I have an idea.

Me: What's that?

God: Climb that tree.

Me: Which one?

God: The tree you just took that picture of.

Me: Uh, that seems a bit scary.

God: Oh, it's going to be.

Me: You are aware of my limited motor skills, right?

God: Very aware. I remember all those smelly elementary school gym classes where you had the coordination of a stick of butter. There is a good chance that you will fall or at least be bitten by a territorial squirrel.

Me: So, why would on Earth would I climb it?!

God: To remind yourself that sometimes you will have to work harder than other people do to feel My light. There are days when you have to fight for yourself. Sometimes My light will easily find you, but at other times, like today, you have to get on your feet and go find it yourself. Climb. Fight. Struggle. Claw. All the way up that tree until you feel the warmth of the sun again. This is your journey.

Me: Sounds like a lot of work.

God: You're worth it.

Me: Depression is the worst.

God: Depression is finite. My love for you is infinite. Do the math. It doesn't stand a chance.

Me: Right.

God: Start climbing. Touch the sun. Feel the light again.

Forgiveness

Me: Hey God.

God: Hey John.

Me: I carry a lot of grudges.

God: I can see that.

Me: When will I learn how to forgive those who have hurt me?

God: When you learn how to ask for forgiveness from all the people that you have hurt.

Me: I've lost so many relationships due to pettiness. I've burned so many bridges. Closed so many doors. Lost so many friends.

God: Most burnt bridges can be rebuilt. Most slammed doors can be unlocked. Most lost friends can be rediscovered. Just take it one sincere atonement at a time. Don't allow words of apology to go unspoken.

Me: Wait – you said MOST bridges can be rebuilt. What about the times when my apology won't be enough to fix things?

God: Let it go. Do your best to make peace with those people to whom you've caused pain. Make peace with Me. Then let it go. Your heart was never made for clinging so tightly to your past mistakes.

Me: What if somebody won't forgive me?

God: They might not. If other people offer you forgiveness, you will ultimately have to learn how to forgive yourself. That's the hardest part. Once you reconcile with yourself, you will learn how to forgive others.

Me: How will that teach me to forgive others?

God: Because once you learn to forgive yourself, forgiving other people is a piece of cake. Free yourself from the chains of resentment and animosity. Ask for forgiveness so you can learn to forgive yourself, and then you can learn how to forgive others.

Me: Saying sorry to everybody that I need to could take a lifetime.

God: I hope your cell phone plan is solid.

I Only Make Oddballs

Me: Hey God.

God: Hey John.

Me: I don't fit in anywhere.

God: Awesome!

Me: I'm an oddball.

God: That's what I like to hear!

Me: I feel like an outsider.

God: Perfect! I'm getting goosebumps here!

Me: I wish I were a little bit more normal.

God: What does "normal" mean?

Me: You know, it means being just like everybody else.

God: Please! Normal doesn't exist. There is no such thing as being normal. I think what you are talking about is conformity and that's the opposite of what I want. I've made individuals, not robots. I've made a billion different colors of human life. I wish you would all quit trying to blend in with each other.

Me: I don't think You're getting what I'm saying.

God: I do. You want an easier life by going with the herd, but that is never going to happen. I want you to honor the individual life that I've given you by wildly embracing your uniqueness. Quit fighting who you are. I want each one of My unique creations to find their inner weirdo and make their mark.

Me: Yeah, that's great, but You made me kind of a super-freak.

God: You're welcome.

Death And Disco

Me: Hey God.

God: Hey John.

Me: I got invited to a disco party next week. I'm excited.

God: Disco? Yuck.

Me: It's great. I've got some sweet moves. I just need to buy some tight pants.

God: No. You really don't have to do that. Besides, disco's dead, Johnny-Boy.

Me: I'm bringing it back. And please, don't use that word.

God: Which one? Dead?

Me: Yeah. I'm afraid of death.

God: Don't be. Death is just a doorway.

Me: I don't want to go through that doorway.

God: You won't have much of a choice.

Me: Why do You let us die?

God: You don't really die.

Me: Our bodies do.

God: That's true.

Me: Why does that have to happen?

God: So that you won't take your life and your relationships on Earth for granted.

Me: I don't do that.

God: Yes, you do. You never think about your own mortality. You never think about death. You think you have time to get everything done. You think that there is always tomorrow to fix relationships. Or to write your book. Or to do whatever. You keep forgetting that the clock is ticking.

Me: That's so scary.

God: It's really not. Death is the best teacher you'll ever have. Imagine how differently you would behave if you believed there was a even a small chance that this could be your last day alive. How would you treat your family? How would you treat the person who made your coffee at Starbucks? How would you have spent your day? Would you have spent your time worrying about ridiculous things? Or would you have focused your energy only on what really matters? Imagine being invested in just the present moment instead of fretting about the past or future. Imagine how often you would have gone outside and spent your time among the flowers and trees. If you thought that today might be your swansong, you wouldn't leave words unsaid. You would tell all those people in your life how much you love them. You would make peace with those that you need to. You would pour out your heart. Plus, if you considered that you might die today, I bet you would have spent more time with Me.

Me: Maybe.

God: No maybe about it. Death is the ultimate reality check. It's meant to keep you all focusing on what is most important. Imagine living a life where every day you woke up and honored it fully since you didn't know if it would be your last. And here's a spoiler: YOU DON'T KNOW. Love, live and serve hard. This could be it.

Me: That's all well and good, but what I really want to know is what will happen to me when I die?

God: You'll join Me on the other side of that doorway that I was talking about.

Me: And what's over there?

God: Eternal peace and love.

Me: What else will be there?

God: Everything.

Me: Everything? Even disco?

God: Eh. Almost everything.

Storms Always Pass

Me: Hey God.

God: Hey John.

Me: Ugh. Can't sleep.

God: You should really try.

Me: That's not going to happen. My mind is racing.

God: Anxiety again?

Me: Yeah.

God: What's up?

Me: My life feels like I'm stuck in the middle of a terrifying storm. Sun is hidden. Rain is pounding. Lightning is crackling. Wind is howling. Thunder is booming. The water is rising.

God: Sounds scary.

Me: It really is. Sometimes I feel like this storm is going to knock down my walls and swallow me up whole.

God: It won't. Just hang on a bit longer. Storms always pass.

Me: Even the big ones?

God: Yep, and guess what the best part is?

Me: What?

God: The bigger and the more severe the thunderstorm, the bigger and more colorful the rainbow afterwards will be.

Me: Good point.

God: Just wait and hold on for it. It's almost here.

Me: It better be one hell of a rainbow...

God: Oh, don't worry. It's going to be glorious.

Wrong Question

Me: Hey God.

God: Hey John.

Me: I need You to answer a question.

God: Sure!

Me: What's going to happen to me when I die?

God: That's not the question you should be asking.

Me: What should I be asking?

God: You should be asking yourself how audaciously you will love while you are alive.

Scream Therapy

Me: Hey God.

God: Hey John.

Me: I'm so stressed out today!

God: Have you heard of Primal Scream Therapy?

Me: No...

God: It's where you think of all of the things in your life that are causing you to suffer and then you just scream it all out of you as loud and as long as you can.

Me: Does that actually work?

God: It has for some people.

Me: I think I'll try it.

God: Nice.

Me: AHHHHHHHHHHHHHHHHHH!!!!!!! (gasp) AAAAAHHHHHHHHHHH!!!!! (gasp) AHHH!!!! AHHHHHHHHHHHHH!!!!!!!! (gasp) AHHHH!!! AHH...

[five minutes later]

Me: AHHHHHHHHHH!!!

God: Wow. That was impressive. Especially all of the dancing that you decided to add to it.

Me: Thanks. It just came over me. I feel a bit dizzy and it looks like I drooled a bit.

God: That's okay. Do you feel better?

Me: Kind of...though I think I scared everyone in the restaurant.

God: Yeah, next time you should definitely do that at home.

The Narrator

Me: Hey God.

God: Hey John.

Me: Why am I so tired all the time?

God: Because you have allowed fear to become the narrator of your story.

Me: That doesn't make any sense.

God: You're always afraid of something. Fear is the most exhausting emotion. If left unchecked, it can paralyze every cell in your body and sap all your energy. Unabated fear is a toxin.

Me: How did I let myself get this way?

God: By letting it stick to your heart. Fear is meant to be a temporary response. It's supposed to pass through you. You were never meant to cling to fear. You allowed terror and despair a seat at your table and fear is the only voice you listen to these days.

Me: I don't know how to get rid of it.

God: Fear is like a stray cat. Quit feeding it. Stop listening to the fearmongers on TV or in your daily life. Be suspicious of people who try to make you be afraid all the time...they are probably just trying to sell you something.

Me: Are you saying that I should never be afraid?

God: No. Fear can be useful, just don't let it linger and dictate all your decisions. Being afraid can be addictive. You should break the habit of being scared all the time.

Me: Easier said than done. The world is a scary place.

God: The world is beautiful. You are just too busy staring at the shadows to notice its many hues. Pay attention to the beauty that surrounds you. It takes more courage to live a life of hope than it does to give in to fear.

Me: I have very little courage, though.

God: That's because you believe your narrator. Fire fear from the role of being your chief storyteller. Find a new voice to listen to.

Me: Whose voice would that be? Yours?

God: Ours. Let's narrate your story together.

Me: I'm not sure that will work.

God: Let's give it a try. Start every sentence with a "Yes, and..."

Me: Okay...

God: The world isn't hopeless.

Me: Yes, and I can be brave in the face of calamity.

God: Yes, and the world is actually very beautiful.

Me: Yes, and people are inherently good.

God: Yes, and you are not alone.

Me: Yes, and love is greater than hate.

God: Yes, and you can live a life of hope.

Me: Yes, and I won't surrender to fear.

God: See! Change the narrator.

Me: And my story will change...

God: Yes, and you are going to be okay.

Me: Yes, and...

Twitter War

Me: Hey God.

God: Hey John.

Me: You're going to be so proud of me.

God: Why is that?

Me: I totally just won a Twitter war!

God: Explain to Me what a Twitter war is again.

Me: It's where two people argue via tweet, back and forth for a couple of hours about some sort of political/religious/sports/pop culture issue.

God: Sounds horrible.

Me: I was amazing! I dominated with both the logic of a physicist and the emotion of a fiery street preacher. There was no stopping me! I was sanctimonious and humbly self-righteous in equal measure in my utter destruction of my enemy.

God: How do you know if you won?

Me: Well, I just kept yammering away until the other person was so worn down that they surrendered to what I was saying and stopped talking.

God: So, you used the same approach you used to convince your wife to marry you.

Me: Pretty much.

Read In Case Of Emergency

Me: Hey God.

Depression: God isn't here. God has abandoned you. You are alone in your suffering.

Me: Hold that thought. God told me to read this letter whenever you showed up again.

UNFOLDS CRINKLED LETTER AND READS IT.

My child,

I'm here. I'm here. I'm here. Right now. I am here. I am present to you. You are not alone. I am here in your tears. I am here with you in your shaking hands. I'm here. I'm here with you in your numb heart and foggy brain. I'm here. Cradling you in my arms. I am here. You are not alone. You are my masterpiece. My treasure. My art. My child. You are My beloved. I am right here. Darkness may surround you but I am the candlelight within you. Nothing can stop Me. I am here. Right now. I am the one stitching your wounds together. We are not separated by your suffering. I'm here with you. Don't despair. Don't listen to the crawling shadow. Listen to Me. I am eternal. Pain is temporary. I am here. I love you. My love for you is older than stardust. You are not alone. I am here. Despair will fade. You will rise. You are not alone. I am here. Right now.

I know it hurts, but don't give up. Fight. Fight. Fight. Fight the darkness. You are not alone. I am here.

Love, God.

Depression: Dang. Whatever. I'm gonna go.

Me: Don't let the door hit ya.

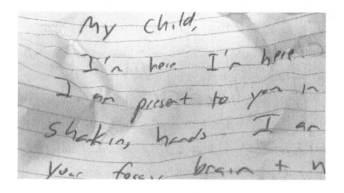

Get Lost. Get Moving.

Me: Hey God.

God: Hey John.

Me: I have no direction in my life.

God: That's okay.

Me: Is it? I'm 42 years old and I don't know where my life is headed.

God: You want to know which way to go?

Me: Yes!

God: Just start heading My way.

Me: Sure... Where are You?

God: I'm everywhere.

Me: That's not super helpful advice...

God: I'm kind of mysterious like that.

Me: Seriously, I am so lost.

God: Awesome! Being lost is the best way to see the world and meet people you wouldn't normally meet. Explore. Move it. Embrace the unknown. Try new roads, even the ones that look scary. The trick is to keep moving. Don't get stuck at a crossroads in your life. You have already wasted so much time trying to decide which possible path is the safest. Quit always trying to be safe. Stop being afraid to fail. Adventures don't happen until you allow them to. Don't be afraid of being lost. It's a gift. It means that you haven't settled for something in your life that you don't feel to be true. Never build your home on sand. Keep moving. Never close your mind to new experiences or new lessons. One of the best parts of being lost is that you will constantly be challenged by experiences that will widen your view of the world I have created for you. Don't miss the millions of opportunities I am going to give you to help other people on the way. Use your gifts to help those who are just as lost as you are.

Remain curious and listen to your heart. Don't allow yourself to stagnate. If you allow your conscience to be your compass and the sound of My voice to be your North Star, you will find your way through the wilderness. Quit standing still because the one thing you can't do is nothing.

Get moving. Get moving. One foot in front of the other. Go somewhere. Get lost. Don't worry about being alone because you never will be. Whichever direction you go, you will have a companion. I'm everywhere. I am in every direction. Get moving. Get moving. Get moving. No more excuses.

Me: That sounds like a typical high school graduation speech. Why can't You just give me a detailed map to show me the way?

God: I just did.

Apples And Trees

Me: Hey God.

God: Hey John.

Me: It's Father's Day.

God: I know. I can't wait to see how many Home Depot gift cards I get. What do you want?

Me: The only gift I want is for the squirrels to quit running across my roof whenever I try to sleep in. They are doing it on purpose.

God: That's what your dad thought too. His relationship with the squirrels was always strained. He was sure they were out to get him.

Me: I forgot all about that. It's funny how we both take nature so personally.

God: The apple doesn't fall far from the tree.

Me: Huh?

God: That means you are a lot like your father. Plus, you two have the exact same eyes. It's uncanny.

Me: To be honest, Father's Day is always kind of hard for me.

God: Why?

Me: Because my dad has been gone for half of my life.

God: He hasn't gone anywhere.

Me: My dad died almost twenty years ago.

God: Death isn't the end. Your dad isn't gone. He lives on in your love of him. Keep his memory alive by remembering all the lessons in kindness that he taught you. Honor his life by giving your children the kind of love that he showed you.

Me: I wish he could have seen me grow up. I wish he could have seen his grandchildren.

God: He has seen it all.

Me: How?

God: Through your eyes. They are exactly like his were. Apples and trees, remember?

Me: Right. I hope he is proud of me.

God: He loves the tree that you've become for your children.

Me: Wait – I'm a tree?

God: Yep.

Me: When did that happen?

God: When you became a dad.

Me: Fatherhood is terrifying.

God: That's what your dad used to say.

Me: Apples and trees?
God: Apples and trees.

Worry Worry Worry

Me: Hey God.

God: Hey John.

Me: I was up all night again. The dark always seems to bring out my deepest anxieties.

God: You worry too much.

Me: I have a lot to worry about.

God: Don't hold on to those worries. Most of the time you worry about things you can't control. Give those worries about ten seconds of your time and then direct your energy to what you can control.

Me: And what is that, exactly?

God: You can control how much you trust in Me, how hard you work to pursue your dreams and how much of your love you share with others. Aside from those things you aren't really in control of anything.

Me: I just don't want bad things to happen to me anymore.

God: You want your life to be perfect?

Me: Yes.

God: Where's the fun in that?

Me: I feel so beaten down.

God: The darkness will pass. You'll rise.

Me: I have too much weighing me down.

God: The darkness will pass. You'll rise.

Me: It's easier to give up.

God: The darkness will pass. You'll rise.

Me: I'm tired of suffering.

God: Spoiler Alert: The darkness will pass. You will rise. I promise.

Me: How do you know?

God: Because I've seen the end of your story. It ends with the words "John died peacefully with a smile on his face and a taco in his hand."

Me: That would be perfect. I love tacos.

God: Who doesn't? Let go of all those worries and get some sleep.

Me: Oh, look the sun is coming up.

God: John, the sun is always coming up. Light always wins. The darkness always passes.

Me: Now what?

God: Now, you rise.

Me: Breakfast tacos?

God: Breakfast tacos!

Complaint Department

Me: Hey God.

God: Hey John.

Me: I have a complaint.

God: Super. What's up?

Me: I went on a walk this morning to clear my head and a bird pooped on me.

God: I know.

Me: You saw it?

God: Of course I did. It wasn't just any bird. It was one of my favorite robins. Her name is Morning Lyric and she has the sweetest song.

Me: I don't care about her singing! Couldn't you have stopped her from ruining my shirt?

God: Sure, but I actually asked her to do it.

Me: What!? Why?!

God: To remind you to be grateful.

Me: You sent a bird to poop on me to remind me to be grateful!? How does that work?!

God: That it wasn't a goose.

Me: Gross!

God: Heh.

Rock Bottom

Me: Hey God.

God: Hey John.

Me: I've hit rock bottom.

God: Great!

Me: Not great. I can't possibly feel any lower than I do right now.

God: That's awesome. Let the healing begin. I brought you a cool miner's hat with a flashlight on it. I bet you'll look like a Minion. Try it on for Me.

Me: No thanks. Can't you just help me make a ladder, so I can climb out of this pit?

God: Not yet. Let's look around for a bit.

Me: Why?

God: Rock bottom is always the best place to start looking for gold.

Me: You are such an optimist.

God: Once you're out of here you're going to be able to turn this whole place into a sweet swimming pool someday.

Me: Thanks for not leaving me alone down here.

God: There's no other place I'd rather be.

Me: You know what? This would also make a good wine cellar.

God: That's the spirit!

Me: The possibilities are endless. I'll take that miner's hat now.

Evolve

Me: Hey God.

God: Hey John.

Me: I'm ready for our relationship to evolve.

God: I'm all for it. Just say the magic words and we can move on to the next stage in our relationship.

Me: Magic words? What are they?

God: I can't tell you because that would ruin it. But once you say them, our whole relationship will transform.

Me: Come on. I'm tired of having to do all this work myself.

God: You'll get there.

Me: Whatever, look... we've been having conversations for well over a year now. I'm ready for the truth. Are You real or not?

God: I'm real.

Me: Show me.

God: Sure. Take a look around you. You are surrounded by the beautiful art of all My creation and more graces than you would ever be able to count. The Earth is jam-packed full of wonder and color. The proof of My existence is in every single one of those brush strokes I have made on the canvas of your world.

Me: Huh. All of that sounds great, but I still don't see anything.

God: That's because your eyes are too tightly shut. Seriously, you have them pinched closed so fiercely that you have this freaky vein sticking out on your forehead.

Me: Go ahead and open my eyes for me.

God: I could do all that...but I'm not going to.

Me: Ugh. Must I do everything myself?!

God: Opening your eyes to behold the miracles that surround you is the very least you can do.

Me: Our relationship is so one-sided!

God: True.

Me: My faith crisis continues.

God: Open your eyes. Open your eyes. Open your eyes. Open your eyes. Open. Your. Eyes. Don't be afraid. Open your -

Me: Fine! I'll take a quick peek.

God: And what do you see?

Me: Everything is so bright. So many swirling colors.

God: Right?!

Me: So beautiful...

God: I do good work.

Me: I'm so grateful. I'm so grateful. I'm so grateful for all that You've made.

God: There are the magic words!

Me: I've never thanked You?

God: Not really.

Me: I feel different.

God: Gratitude is life changing. The more you embrace gratitude and the more keep your eyes open to the wonders I have created, the more real I'll become in your life.

Me: There are so many colors...

God: Yeah, I'm a pretty good artist. I love coming up with new colors that nobody has ever seen before.

Me: Now what?

God: Now you can help me paint. It's going to be awesome!

Me: Thank you.

God: I can't hear that enough!

Some Perspective

Me: Hey God.

God: Hey John.

Me: Thanks for meeting me for lunch.

God: You bet. Did you order yourself a salad?

Me: Kind of. I ordered a double chili cheeseburger.

God: That is pretty much the opposite of a salad.

Me: It comes with onions, so it's kind of like a salad.

God: You have a hairy face, but that doesn't make you a lumberjack.

Me: Huh?

God: Never mind, here's your food.

Me: Gross! They put sliced TOMATOES on top of it!

God: Yum!

Me: I hate tomatoes!

God: Wait, aren't there tomatoes in chili anyway? What is the problem?

Me: That's way different. I like my tomatoes pureed. Not whole like this. This is outrageous! I told them no tomatoes!!

God: Are you crying?

Me: Maybe! I'm going to freak out! How could they do this to me!?

God: I'm sure it was an honest mistake.

Me: Oh no! This goes beyond being just "a mistake". This is another example of how nobody ever listens to me.

God: I think this is just an example of somebody accidentally putting tomatoes on your food. All you have to do is use your fork to take the tomatoes off of your plate.

Me: Nothing ever goes my way...

God: You may need to consider the possibility that you are overreacting right now.

Me: I'm suffering!

God: No, you're not. You are misusing that word because you lack perspective.

Me: I don't know how to change my perspective!

God: John, you live on a rocky planet that is rotating around a sun in a vast solar system that is part of the Milky Way galaxy. There are over 400 million solar systems like yours in the Milky Way and there are hundreds of millions of other galaxies in the known universe. This means that there are around a septillion other suns out there, which suggests there are well over 1,000,000,000,000,000,000,000,000 planets in your observable universe. Your little rocky planet is just one of them. It's a tiny bit of dust floating among an infinite sea of other tiny bits of dust in a universe that is 14 billion years old.

On your little piece of dust that is floating in that infinite and ancient universe, there are billions of people scurrying around. Some of these people are okay, but many are not and they are suffering. There are uncountable reasons for why people suffer. There are unjust wars and genocide. There is famine, disease, poverty, religious persecution, natural disasters, family strife and hatred. There is real suffering out there. Not just on your planet, but throughout the infinite universe. I hear everybody's cries of heartache and grief. I've heard them all through history and I hear them today.

Me: And?

God: Well, in that context, your melodramatic reaction to a few misplaced tomatoes on your lunch plate doesn't classify as actual suffering.

Me: That's a good point. I'm sorry. I often lose sight of things. I'll just take them off my plate.

God: No harm done. Now, we need to talk about–

Me: Wait, what are those?

God: Oh no…

Me: Are those pickles??! Gross!!!

God: Remember to have perspect–

Me: PICKLES!!!!!!!!

God: I guess you are kind of having a salad after all.

Weaponized Religion

Me: Hey God.

God: Hey John.

Me: Why does it seem like so many of the people who brag about their intimate understanding of You turn out to be so incredibly cruel?

God: It's been like that for thousands of years. There have always been those who have used My Name to hurt or scare others.

Me: I can't imagine it's easy for You to see.

God: I wish those people would choose kindness over self-righteousness, and empathy over judgment. Love over division.

Me: Can't You just talk some sense into those who claim to be so incredibly close to You and then use it as an excuse to purposely wound other people?

God: I would love to, but most of the time they haven't ever actually spoken to Me. They just talk about Me.

Me: Then how do they know You?

God: Exactly.

On Repeat

Me: Hey God.

God: Hey John.

Me: Why do I keep making the same mistakes over and over?

God: Because you keep pressing the repeat button on them.

Me: Why would I do that?

God: You don't believe that you can ever change and grow as a person.

Me: I don't?

God: You have chosen to take the easy road of living a life where you are stuck in an ugly pattern of self-inflicted suffering because you never allow yourself to learn from your mistakes.

Me: I was hoping you were going to say something a little more upbeat.

God: Like what?

Me: Something like "Hang in there!" or " You're doing great!" And then after we'd hug it out and go eat some cookies.

God: The truth is you're not doing that great. You've bought into what that horrible voice in your head has said about your inability to become a different person. You believe that ridiculous voice when it tells you that you will always be stuck with making the same bad choices because that is who you are. You've just accepted that you are a prisoner to the person that you are right now and that you can never transform your life for the better.

Me: I'm not sure I can change who I am at this point.

God: Of course you can, if you are willing to put in some hard work. Because learning to ignore what that voice in your head is telling you will take some hard work. That's why you resist doing what's required of you. It takes great effort to forgive yourself for your past blunders and decide to change. You're a spiritual sloth. Time to put the labor in, Johnny-Boy. It's well past time to expect more out of yourself.

Me: Are You suggesting that if I change as a person, I won't make any more mistakes?

God: Quite the opposite. You are going to make some great, big, juicy mistakes in your future.

Me: Ugh.

God: Yup, you will be making some monster, headline-making screw-ups. In fact, your future humongous mistakes will be made into ballads and sung as cautionary tales about what not to do.

Me: I got it...yeesh.

God: Just learn from them. Allow yourself to fail spectacularly and then learn from it. Refuse the temptation to listen to the voice inside your head. Forgive yourself and know that you can change. You can end your suffering by releasing your old patterns of thought and behavior. Quit pressing repeat on your mistakes.

Me: It's not too late for me to become a different kind of person?

God: If you're breathing there is still plenty of time to become the person I made you to be. You are not the product of all your past mistakes, you are the promise of all the infinite joy that lies in front of you. Just have the courage to shut up the negative voice in your head and start making new choices. Quit pressing repeat on the same old mistakes.

Me: I'm on it! I'm going to change my life!

God: Awesome! Break those patterns!

Me: Starting tomorrow...or possibly next Monday...

God: Quit pressing repeat on the same old mistakes...

Me: Right. Okay, how about I start right after lunch?

God: Fine. I'll take it what I can get.

Me: Hug it out and cookies?

God: Bring it on.

Rockslide

Me: Hey God.

God: Hey John.

Me: How can I help my autistic son?

God: By helping him to dig past the rockslide that has separated the two of you.

Me: You've noticed? I'm just worried that autism has buried him so deeply that I won't ever be able to reach him.

God: Your son is amazing. You shouldn't worry about him.

Me: But it has to be so cold and dark underneath all of those heavy rocks covering him. I need to get him out!

God: No you don't. He isn't in darkness. Your son is in a world of color and energy. He is living in a garden of glorious flowers and light. Of compassion and grace. Of dreams and hope. Of rhythm and melody. Of wonder and resurrection. Your son is flourishing in that garden. He isn't beneath the rocks of the autism landslide. He made it out before he was buried.

Me: He did?!

God: Yes. But you didn't.

Me: I'm not the one who was swept away in the rockslide.

God: Yes, you are. Autism was never the avalanche; your grief towards his diagnosis was. You're the one who has been trapped under the rubble for years.

Me: What are you talking about?! I would have known if that had happened to me!

God: You just got too used to being buried to see what had happened to you. You've become comfortable being entombed within despair and worry. You have allowed yourself to be buried by his autism. While you've been there among the rocks, your son has been out here with Me. We've been growing the most amazingly vibrant garden anybody has ever seen.

Me: I can't get out. These rocks are too heavy.

God: Only because you've let so many of them build up. You never dealt with any of your pain or grief so they have burgeoned. It's time to push your way out. Your son has been waiting for you.

Me: I can't believe that he never gave up on me...

God: When he isn't growing his garden, he has been busy trying to dig you out. He has so much to show you. Your son never deserted you, even after you surrendered to worry and sadness. He just kept digging for you. Look through the tiny cracks between the rocks and you'll see his hand reaching for you.

Me: I still don't understand why this all happened in the first place. This could have all be avoided. Why did you allow him to have autism?

God: To teach the world that the most beautiful flowers can still bloom even after earthquakes, rockslides and avalanches. There is no avoiding heartbreak in life. There is just the choice not to allow yourself to be buried alive by it.

Me: I can't wait to see his garden.

God: He can't wait to show you. It's wonderful.

Me: Different isn't broken.

God: Different is beautiful.

Me: Life is too short to cling to heartache.

God: Don't choose suffering. Don't choose a life among the rocks.

Me: Choose joy. Choose the garden.

God: If you ever get buried, just start digging. Don't stop. Keep digging. Look for the spaces between the rocks and the dirt. There will be hands in there to help pull you out. Just keep digging.

Me Keep digging.

Please Don't

Me: Hey God.

God: Hey John.

Me: I quit.

God: Please don't.

Me: I am giving up all hope that I'm ever going to feel better again.

God: Please don't.

Me: I want to surrender to the gaping emptiness inside of me.

God: Please don't.

Me: I want to stop talking to You.

God: Please don't.

Me: But I've reached my breaking point.

God: You're not breaking. You're just bending. It hurts so much because you are stretching. Stretching hurts.

Me: So, this is like some sort of extreme spiritual yoga?

God: Yes, kind of, I suppose.

Me: That's cool. I've always wanted to squeeze into some yoga pants!

God: Please don't.

Me: Uh oh. The pants got stuck on my luxuriantly upholstered thighs. Can You help me get them–

God: PLEASE DON'T!!!!

This Isn't A War

Me: Hey God.

God: Hey John.

Me: I'm losing my battle with depression today.

God: Is that why you're still in bed?

Me: Yeah. I'm not getting out.

God: Come on. Get up.

Me: No. I'm overwhelmed.

God: Just put your feet on the floor and take one step at a time.

Me: I can't.

God: Your day can get started with just one little step.

Me: Not gonna happen. Depression has won the fight this morning.

God: I think it's time to stop treating your experience with depression like a war.

Me: You want me to give up?

God: I want you to change your perspective on what's happening to you. For you, there is no cure for depression. There is no war to be won. There will never be a day when you and depression aren't intertwined. It's time for you to understand that depression will always be a part of you. You must be exhausted from fighting it all the time.

Me: I am.

God: Then quit resisting it. Instead of waging a war with depression, you should negotiate a ceasefire. It's impossible to rid yourself of it completely, so make it your dance partner instead of your foe.

Me: I can't believe you want me to surrender...

God: Not surrender. I want you to accept its place in your daily life. Instead of allowing whether or not you are winning or losing your war with depression to dictate your mood every day, find a way to coexist peacefully with it.

Me: That's impossible! This is a war! Only one of us is going to win! It's either depression or me!

God: But the depression IS you. You are at war with yourself. You are resisting a part of yourself. It's futile.

Me: I don't want to feel this way anymore. It's not that I feel sad. It's just that I feel profoundly empty, which is far worse. I'm numb. I'd take sadness over this feeling any day. Can't You just take this away from me?

God: This is your journey. This is your story. This is what you are meant to experience. This depression can be a gift if you learn from it. It can help you to learn how to help other people on the same path. Why would I take that opportunity away from you? I know it is miserable right now but eventually you will find that there was a purpose and a meaning to your suffering.

Me: That doesn't make me feel any better right now.

God: Tell you what. Just for today, quit trying to fight your depression. Let it come. Don't deny it. Don't fight. Dance with it. Instead of attempting to defeat depression, try to understand it. What is it trying to tell you? What can you do to lighten its grip on you? I'll be right there with you to help you find peace with it. Just for today, approach your depression with an olive branch instead of a sword.

Me: I'll try. But I think I'd rather fight it.

God: Seek a balance with it, rather than fighting it.

Me: I'm a terrible dancer.
God: Just put both feet on the floor and then take one little step at a time.

Courage Isn't A Buzzword

Me: Hey God.

God: Hey John.

Me: Help me! I'm so afraid!

God: No more of that talk. I created you with enough bravery inside of you to face any situation. You just need to tap into that courage.

Me: That is kind of impossible right now!

God: Don't say that. Being courageous takes some practice. You're surrounded by opportunities every day to choose bravery instead of fear.

Me: Look, God, I don't think you understand! There's a –

God: Of course I understand. Allowing fear to rule your life is easy. It's the safe path. We have been over and over this before.

Me: Listen –

God: No, you listen. Enough excuses. It's time for you to become a joyful and bold warrior. Once you stop giving in to fear and start using the courage that I've already given you, everything in your life will change. I know it's hard to be brave:

It takes courage to believe in the goodness of humankind.

It takes courage to have faith that you were born with a purpose.

It takes courage to fight hate with love.

It takes courage to believe in the unseen.

It takes courage to stand up for what you think is right, especially when it is against popular sentiment.

It takes courage to not give up on yourself.

It takes courage to forgive those who do evil.

It takes courage to be willing to fail.

It takes courage to sing a song of peace instead of joining in with the drumbeats of war.

It takes courage to tell your story.

It takes courage to admit to your weaknesses and mistakes.

It takes courage to surrender to the things in your life that you can't control.

It takes courage to tune out the voice in your head telling you that you're not good/smart/beautiful enough.

It takes courage to be creative and to reflect the artistry that I so carefully used in forming you.
It takes courage to find more value in serving other people than yourself.
It takes courage to throw out your life map when it is no longer leading you to where you want to go.
It takes courage to step off of the road and start to explore the wilderness of your heart.
It takes courage to be still and listen for My voice during the raging storm.
It takes courage to release unhealthy relationships in which you feel bad about yourself.
It takes courage to demand better friends in your life.
It takes courage to turn away from whatever encourages self-destructive behavior in your life.
It takes courage not to ignore the cries of the poor.
It takes courage to be merciful.
It takes courage to allow yourself to be happy.
It takes courage to not respond to hateful rhetoric with some of your own.

*It takes courage to wait for the light of dawn
during the darkest of night.
It takes courage to ask other people for help.
It takes courage to live joyfully even amid
suffering and grief.
It takes courage to believe in miracles!
It takes courage to believe in peace!
It takes courage to believe in love!
It takes courage to believe in My hope!
It takes courage to believe in Me!*

You already have the courage to do all these things! Find the bravery that I've given you and USE it! It will all be worth it! Your life will transform and you will become the person that I made you to be!

Your heart is ready to be ignited by the fires of courage and bravery! There is plenty of kindling inside of you to light this fire. You are ready to live fearlessly. Be daring! Be audacious! Use the courage that is welled up inside of you!

Me: I can't!

God: Even after all that I have said? You still can't find the courage inside of you? What are you so afraid of?

Me: I've been trying to tell you! There is a huge wasp sitting on my face!! It's been there for the last two minutes!

God: Oh, yeah. It looks really mad. I think it's attracted to your whimpering.

Me: Any advice?

God: Sometimes it takes courage to be stung on your forehead and then openly cry in front of your children.

Me: Great...

God: Bee not afraid.

Me: Ugh.

God: Get it? Bee?

Me: Yes...I get it.

God: Heh.

Evening Prayers

Me: Hey God.

God: Hey John.

Me: The sun has set.

God: Yep. You should say an evening prayer.

Me: I can't focus. My anxiety is at its worst at night.

God: Why do you think that is?

Me: I think it's because I don't know what will happen to me tomorrow. It's the uncertainty of the future that terrifies me the most.

God: Do you want me to go ahead and tell you what is going to happen to you tomorrow?

Me: Yes, please!

God: You will be loved. You will be wrapped in love.

Me: Always?

God: Always.

Me: The sun has set.

God: Yet, you are still surrounded by light.

Me: Will you stay with me while I sleep?

God: Always.

No Ordinary Days

Me: Hey God.

God: Hey John.

Me: Good morning.

God: Good morning!

Me: Ick. Another ordinary day...

God: No, it's not! This is an extra-special-amazing kind of a day!

Me: Awesome! I can't face the prospect of another boring day. What is going on today?

God: Let's see. I have a crazy schedule all lined up for you! Today you are going to be living on a rocky planet that is orbiting a giant fireball while hurtling through a chaotic and infinite space. You get to be a passenger on this celestial trolley as you cruise through the solar system. Tonight, you will be able to sit in a hilltop and watch as the stars float across your horizon. I put them there just for you! It's going to be epic!

Me: Uh-huh. What else?

God: Today on your little rocky planet you will be interacting with billions of other people who are scrambling around frantically to do things like make money, fall in love or find the answer to why I put them there in the first place. There will be people everywhere! You will be given countless opportunities to serve these folks and show them mercy, love and grace. Some people will inspire and move you, while others will disappoint you and break your heart. A roller coaster of interactions and emotions awaits you! I'm getting goosebumps thinking about it!

Me: Yeah...what else?

God: You will also be surrounded by the beauty and wonder of My creation. All day long! You won't be able to miss it. I've made a dazzling world for you to explore! There will be trees! Butterflies! Flowers! Dogs! Even a rainbow! And at some point you're going to be pooped on by a yellow-headed bird! Wild, huh?

Me: Um. Gross. What else?

God: Best of all, today is going to feature a series of moments where you will be confronted with the opportunity finally to let go of all of your fears and doubts. You'll be given the choice to focus on life instead of grief. Hope over despair!

Today you'll be able to spend some time with Me so that you can come to know how much I love you and how many plans I have for your life.

Me: Right...but...

God: But what? Today is going to be an amazing once-in-lifetime kind of a day! It's going to be a rodeo of sights, sounds, joy and adventure!

Me: But...everything you've mentioned exists or is possible every day.

God: Exactly! And you've been missing out. Time to join the party. It's all there waiting for you. Life is too short not to embrace the adventure and possibilities that surround you.

Me: I could use an adventure.

God: That's the spirit! Wake up and start owning the life I've given you!

Me: I'm ready – but still, I'm a little bummed out.

God: Why?

Me: Because You said this wasn't going to be an ordinary day.

God: Oh, it's not.

Me: What's going to be so different about it?

God: You. You are going to be different.

Lost Hope (Again)

Me: Hey God.

God: Hey John.

Me: I've lost hope.

God: No, you haven't.

Me: Uh, yes, I have.

God: It's not possible to lose hope. Hope is constant. You can only choose to surrender to despair and ignore the signs of hope that are all around you.

Me: I'm not choosing to feel this way! The world is so relentlessly violent and destructive. Every day there is another story depicting an act of evil that causes the despair to soak into me. I can't help surrendering to being hopeless when every news cycle is full of hate and division. It's unavoidable!

God: I know it's hard to see it now, but eventually the world will know peace.

Me: That's easy for You to say. It seems to me that we are all being swallowed up by a hungry shadow.

God: Shadows are a sign of hope.

Me: What?

God: Shadows don't exist without a light. Hope is always working on washing away the darkness. Quit wasting your life on the passing shadows and focus on the source of light blazing right behind them.

Me: I just wish that light would get here already.

God: Listen to me. The shadows are proof that the light is already here.

Me: I want to believe that.

God: You've become too used to seeing in the dark. Don't be obsessed with the news. Trust in what your heart is trying to tell you:

People are good.
The world is beautiful.
Shadows have an expiration date.
My Light is unending and it is already here.
Shadows are on the run.
Peace will have its say.

Me: It's hard to have hope.

God: Then don't have hope. Let hope have you. Give in to it. Believe that there will never be a time in your life when hope won't be following right behind you.

Me: Never?

God: Never.

Me: The light is coming? Are You sure?

God: Dude, it's already here!

Macho Leak

Me: Hey God.

God: Hey John.

Me: I don't think I can handle talking with You today. I'm too overcome with stress.

God: Is that why you're crying?

Me: I'm not crying. I'm just leaking macho.

God: Uh, sure. It's okay...you don't have to say anything. We can just sit quietly together.

Me: Without talking?

God: Yep.

Me: I don't think that will work for me.

God: Why?

Me: Silence makes me uncomfortable.

God: Just because you aren't talking doesn't mean that there will be silence.

Me: I don't understand?

God: Sometimes when you allow yourself to be fully quiet you can finally hear the lyrics I've been singing to you this whole time.

Me: I didn't know that You were a musician.

God: Of course, I am. There is music in everything that I do. My Creation has a fusion jazz vibe. My grace for you during times of pain sounds just like a piano. When you are lost, I play the loudest drumbeat to help you find your way back home. Everything I do for you is a love song.

Me: How can I hear it?

God: Just be still. Just close your eyes and listen.

Me: I'll try.

God:

Me:

God:

Me:

God:

Me:

God: ☐ ♪ Don't give up. Every little broken piece of you will heal. You will survive this pain. ♪

Me:

God: ☐♫ I've made you for more than suffering. I created you to do great things. Trust me. Trust me. Trust me. ♫

Me:

God: □ ♪ You are loved. I forgive you. Forgive yourself. You are loved. ♪

Me:

God: □ ♪ I believe in you. I'm holding your hand. You are not alone. ♪

Me:

God: □♫ Everything will be okay. Tomorrow will be better. I'm already there. I'm waiting for you in tomorrow to show you all the amazing things that I have in store for you. ♫

Me:

God: □ ♪ Be still. Be still. Quiet your mind. Listen to my love song for you. Be still. Listen. ♪

Me: Thank you...

God: You're leaking macho again.

Photobomber

Me: Hey God.

God: Hey John.

Me: You were right. Getting out into nature was good for me.

God: It's always good to unplug from the world and spend some time in My splendor.

Me: It was cool but I'm pretty sure I saw The Blair Witch.

God: That was just another hiker. She was really confused why you were hiding from her. Her name is Donna. Super nice.

Me: And I saw a chupacabra.

God: It was a log.

Me: A scary log!

God: Right.

Me: I took a cool selfie while I was out there on the cliff.

Me: One thing – why did You photobomb it?

God: Because I'm awesome.

Act III:
Hey God,
I can't do this
anymore.

I want nothing more than to quit
these daily conversations with God.
We are digging into parts of myself that I prefer
to keep buried.
Depression.
Doubt.
Fear.
Anger.
Hopelessness.
Autism.
Each post becomes more and more personal.
Where is this all going?
For the first time in a long time I feel as if God
can see me.

I feel terrified and comforted in equal measure.

"One of the deepest longings of the human soul is to be seen."
—John O'Donohue

Exit Interview

Me: Hey God.

God: Hey John.

Me: I'm still not talking to you.

God: You're not?

Me: No.

God: What is this then?

Me: This is Your exit interview.

God: I see. How have you been?

Me: I'm the one asking the questions today.

God: Gotcha.

Me: I'm going to ask You a few questions, so I can get a better understanding of why our relationship had soured to the point of near collapse. I would appreciate it if You would answer with either a "Yes" or a "No". Okay?

God: I'll try my best. Go ahead.

Me: Do You feel like You are in touch with the needs of the people that You have created?

God: Yes, very much so.

Me: Don't You see that we are suffering down here?

God: First of all, there is no such thing as "down here". I am everywhere. I'm not above you. I'm right here with you, exactly where you are. And yes, of course, I am fully aware of any suffering.

Me: Please keep Your answers to yes or no.

God: Right.

Me: Since You have acknowledged that You are aware of the pain and turmoil that exists, don't You feel like it is Your job to put an end to it?

God: I don't have a job.

Me: Is that a "no?"

God: It's a firm "no". I didn't create people to avoid suffering. I created humankind to come to know Me through the joys and anguish that come with being of flesh and bone. The pain and loss you experience isn't for Me to take away. I would be robbing you if I did.

Me: I don't think I would miss the hurt. I don't understand why Your will would be for us to suffer. Wouldn't it be easier to believe in You if there were more intervention on Your part?

God: No. It actually makes it harder. I want people to come to me of their own volition. Not because they see Me floating around on a cloud handing out miracles and healings so they come to kiss My divine behind. I gave you free will to choose to look for Me or to not. I don't want you to have to love Me. I want you to make the choice to.

Me: I don't have room on my sheet for that whole answer. Again, You need to just answer with a yes or no. I don't think I've missed these lectures of Yours very much.

God: I think you have.

Me: Do you feel like You could have done more to help nurture a relationship with me?

God: Aside from breathing life into you, giving you a supportive family, revealing Myself to you through the people you've met, being there for you when the darkness came to take you, surrounding you with awesome nature on an amazing planet swimming in an ocean of an endless universe, all while listening to your nonsensical rants and complaints about the job I'm doing? You mean, do I feel like I could have done more to help you to know Me, despite all of those things that I just mentioned?

Me: Uh...yes.

God: No.

Me: You aren't giving me the answers I was hoping You were going to.

God: That is totally classic God and John, isn't it?

Me: Yeah it is.

God: Can I ask you a yes or no question now?

Me: I guess.

God: Are you going to forgive yourself?

Me: For what?

God: If you have to ask, that means you aren't ready to yet.

Me: Dang.

God: Can I ask you one more yes or no question?

Me: Yes. But then I have to go.

God: Do you miss me?

Me: Maybe.

God: Yes or no.

Me: Yes.

God: I knew it!

Me: This concludes my exit interview.

God: Talk to you tomorrow?

Me: Maybe.

God: Yes or no.

Me: Yes.

God: You bring the coffee.

Me: What are You going to bring?

God: The donuts...

Me: Okay. Make sure mine has strawberry jelly.

God: Do you want to know why I choose to bring donuts? Because they're so hole-y.

Me: Wow.

God: Get it? Donuts have holes in them. They're holy. Get it?

Me: This is the worst exit interview ever.

God: Or the best...

Wildflowers

Me: Hey God.

God: Hey John.

Me: My son was diagnosed with autism thirteen years ago this month.

God: That was an amazing day!

Me: No, it wasn't! I was devastated. I still remember sitting in that uncomfortable chair with the fluorescent light flickering above me while the doctor gave us the results from the tests they had spent all day giving my child.

God: You were so pale.

Me: That's because a stranger in a white coat upended our entire lives in just a few sentences. The doc said, "Your son is autistic." I felt every cell in my body start to pull apart from each other. It was the very beginning of my coming undone.

God: Not that you can remember, but I was there with you in that room at that exact moment.

Me: I didn't think we were talking during that time in my life.

God: Correction: You weren't talking to Me. I was still trying to get through to you but you weren't too interested in what I had to say.

Me: How could I? There was nothing You could say that could have brought me back from the edge. I was devastated. It felt like I was breaking apart on the inside during the two-hour drive home. It was almost a miracle that I didn't just give up right then and there in the car.

God: There is no "almost" about it. There was a miracle taking place.

Me: The only thing I remember about the drive home was that I felt so completely helpless about finding a way to fix my son who was struggling with autism. I was grieving for him like he had died, while he was sitting right behind me in the back seat! Every single plan I had made for my family evaporated in one day. No miracle was taking place in that moment!

God: Sure, there was. I had finally found a way to get through to you.

Me: How?

God: Through a simple smile. It started a chain reaction.

Me: A smile?

God: Don't you remember that moment on the drive home when you turned around to look at your son and he flashed that smile? He was nonverbal at the time, but in that simple smile he told you everything that you needed to know about what was going to happen over the next thirteen years.

Me: That's right, I remember that now. I couldn't believe that he was so happy after such a long day of doctors and specialists. He was smiling from ear to ear.

God: With that smile he instructed you in the way of the joyful warrior. Yes, there were some serious obstacles and suffering ahead, but nothing that would change his heart. In that smile he reminded you that autism might be able to coil around his body but it was never going to be able touch his soul. Autism could try whatever tricks it wanted but it would always be powerless to stop his radiant smile.

Me: I recall feeling strangely relieved when I turned back around in my seat.

God: That's because you felt the spark of joy. Joy is a flame that can't be extinguished, even amid grief and pain.

Me: He's never really stopped smiling. Even after these years.

God: Of course not. It has been his mission to prove to the world that joy can push up through the cracks of a concreted heart, foggy mind or a ravaged body. Joy is like a wildflower that grows on a sidewalk. It always finds a way out.

Me: You're right. That was an amazing day. I remember now that it was later that night that I started talking to You again.

God: Yep. You had been tossing and turning all night. Finally, you whispered to Me "God, help me find the courage to be as happy as my autistic son." It was the first time you had spoken to Me in years.

Me: Things were different for me after that.

God: That one smile had started a chain reaction inside of you. If your son could find the courage to live joyfully...

Me: So could I.

God: Indeed.

Me: Different isn't broken...
God: It's beautiful, like a wildflower.
Me: Joy always finds a way out.

How Long?

Me: Hey God.

God: Hey John.

Me: How long have You loved me?

God: Long before you were born.

Me: Wow.

God: I know, right?! So you had better get to work.

Me: At what?

God: Catching up.

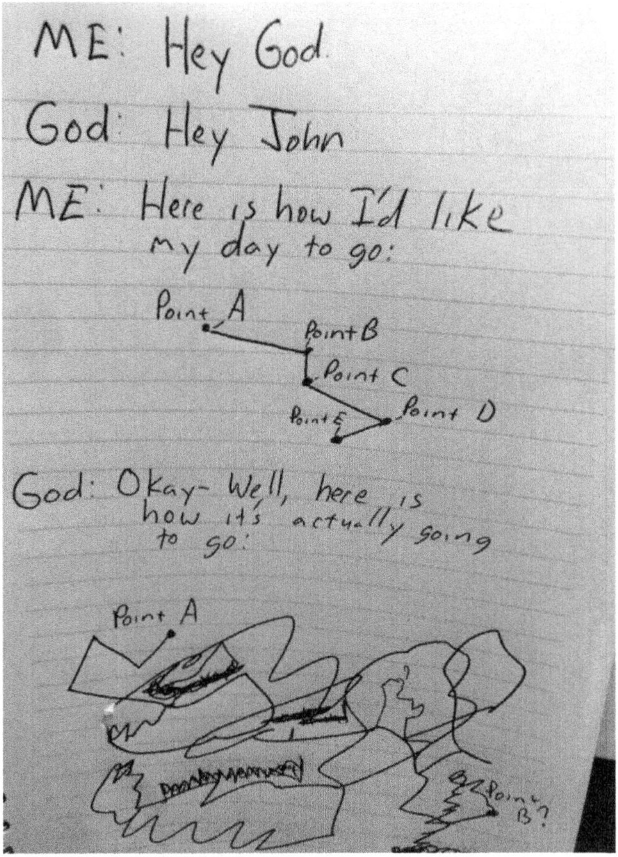

ME: Hey God.
God: Hey John
ME: Here is how I'd like my day to go:
Point A
Point B
Point C
Point D
Point E
God: Okay- Well, here is how it's actually going to go:
Point A
Point B?

This

Me: Hey God.

God: Hey John.

Me: I'm not sure about these posts any more.

God: Why?

Me: Because I think that I'm a fraud. I post our conversations every day yet I'm still plagued with doubts.

God: Relax. Faith is a process. You're just getting started.

Me: You don't think it's a problem that I have so many questions?

God: Nope. I'd be more worried if you didn't have any questions at all.

Me: But my doubts are so great.

God: I am greater than any doubt you'll ever have.

Me: I'm a hypocritical mess.

God: That's okay. I love a challenge.

Me: Why is believing in You so much easier for other people?

God: It isn't easy for anybody. Just don't give up. Keep sharing your life with Me. Be present. Don't check out. Ask the tough questions. It's okay. Some doubts will untangle themselves the more we talk and some new ones will knot up from time to time. It's all part of your faith journey. Besides, maybe there is something good that has come from all of your doubting.

Me: What's that?

God: This.

To Love. To Love. To Love.

Me: Hey God.

God: Hey John.

Me: When did my life get so off track?

God: The moment you stopped living your purpose.

Me: Which is what?

God: Your purpose was to love every little bit of yourself. To love all of your talents and imperfections. To love each chapter of your story equally. To honor the heartaches, the victories, the grief, and the countless graces that fill your pages. You are an original piece of priceless artwork. There will never be another you. Never devalue yourself. You are a unique being in this vast universe.

You were meant to love other people, even those who hate you. You can't be the one that decides who deserves your compassion and understanding and who does not. That doesn't mean surrendering to negative or destructive people, but don't pay back hate with hate. Forgive. Find a way to serve others without ego.

You were meant to love the Earth. There is creation and life exploding all around you. It is the canvas that I'm painting on. The stars, the rocks, the rivers, the lilacs, the critters, the colors, the oceans...all of it is there to remind you about the power of creativity. Everything that I've made for you is marked with My initials. You exist in My living, breathing masterpiece.

You were meant to love this moment you're in right now. Not to allow yourself to be imprisoned by your regrets from yesterday or to become obsessed with an uncertain tomorrow. In this exact moment there is oxygen passing through your lungs and you are surrounded by miracles. Be present in the now. Be grateful for all that is before you in this moment.

I meant for you to love all these things – and many more! – for the gifts that they are. That's your purpose.

Me: Huh. That explanation was a little too complicated for me to remember.

God: You want me to simplify it all?

Me: That'd be great. What's my purpose?

God: To love. That's it. To love. To love. To love.

Me: I better write that down.

When Does Grief Go Away?

Me: Hey God.

God: Hey John.

Me: When will I ever get over grieving the death of someone that I love?

God: Never. Grief doesn't end. It doesn't come and go like a summer storm. It's in the air around you. Grief is permanent. That feeling of loss doesn't have a deadline; it's a wound that becomes the aching scar. When somebody you love dies, it feels as if you have lost a limb. Even years later there can be phantom pains that can bring you to your knees. When you're alive on Earth, grief will always be with you in one form or another.

Me: That's terrible. I'd like to move on now. It's been years.

God: There is no moving on. There is no "getting over" the death of a beloved. Why would you want to? These death pangs that hit you out of the blue are a sign of something wonderful. It means that you have loved somebody so much that their absence in your life is still so felt deeply. Grieving is a profound human experience. It means that you have given a piece of your heart to someone else.

Me: But when that person passes away that piece goes with them.

God: That's the debt you must pay for taking the risk to love somebody else. You are sending your heart to heaven one little bit at a time. You are joining eternity piecemeal. That part of your love for them has moved on with that person when they die, but it's not gone forever! When you join those you have lost in the great beyond one day, you will reclaim all of the pieces that went ahead of you. Eventually, your heart will be whole again. I promise.

Me: It's hard when a wave of emotion pass over me unexpectedly. Sometimes it's triggered by something so small. A scent, a song on the radio, or a random memory popping up in my head. Without warning I'm suddenly overcome with grief.

God: That is the way grief works. Like I told you, grief never leaves you. If you keep the memory of your loved one in your heart, grief will be always lurking. I'm glad that you used the word "wave" earlier because that's exactly how grief works. Grief is a tide. Some days the tide is high. Some days the tide is low. Either way, it's always there on your shore.

Me: If that's true, how do You expect me to function?

God: Because you owe it to the ones that you have lost to live life to its fullest. You can honor their lives by living yours with wild abandon. If you were to die today, you wouldn't want those who love you to give up and quit. You would want your survivors to keep on keepin' on, right?

Me: Right.

God: Good. Look, grief doesn't always mean being sad. Grief can arrive equally as laughter or anger. It is more than a single emotional response. To lament the loss of someone means celebrating their life by cherishing and clinging to those memories with them like prized treasures. Grief doesn't require you to cry. The only requirement that grief has for you is not to close the door on your love for those who have passed away. Keep their memory alive.

Me: This would all be easier for us to understand if You didn't allow death in the first place. You put amazing people in my life and then You take them away. Just like that they are gone.

God: Just because your beloved has died, it doesn't mean that they are gone. They are waiting for you across the veil. Love doesn't go away when the body fails. Love is everlasting. Shared love is immortal. Your grief is just honoring that love. The way of life is to love and be loved so deeply that someday people will profoundly grieve your passing.

Me: Death is so scary. I'm terrified of the end.

God: Johnny-Boy, death is just the beginning.

Me: Of what?

God: Your adventures.

Fog

Me: Hey God.

God: Hey John.

Me: My brain is so foggy this morning.

God: I can see that.

Me: I've been so patient. It's time for You to take away my depression. I've had enough. I've served my time. I want out of this fog.

God: I know you do.

Me: You know, the worst part of being depressed is the time that I waste. I waste time being stuck on a couch or in my bed. I waste time trapped in my mind. Even during the times when I'm not feeling the weight of my depression, I'm wasting time thinking about it. Worrying about when depression's stinger will fill me with its venom again. There is no escape. My life is being squandered in this fog.

God: I need you to trust in Me. I'm going to get you through this. My hand in yours. Together. I'll lead you out into the light.

Me: I just need you to fix me!

God: You aren't broken. You're just human. Don't surrender to your imperfections. Don't give in to your suffering. The fog will lift. The clouds will break. They always do.

Me: But it will come back again...

God: Yes. And when it does, we'll do what we always do. We'll hold hands and wait for breaks in the clouds. And wait for the light to pour out.

Me: Why did You make me like this?

God: Like what?

Me: Depressed?

God: I don't see depression when I look at you.

Me: What do you see?

God: Resilience. You're not defective. This suffering is all a part of your story. The story of how you survived. The story of how the clouds broke all around you.

Me: Fog's lifting!

God: Do want Me to let go of your hand?

Me: Not just yet.

We're Tight!

Me: Hey God.

God: Hey John.

Me: I thought we were getting along?!

God: We are. This is the most we have spoken since you were a kid. Your relationship with Me is growing every day. We are getting super tight!

Me: Okay, so, if we are SO tight then why do You keep letting bad things happen to me?!

God: Because you like to think of Me like I'm an umbrella that will always protect you from every single storm.

Me: That would be great. Let's go with that.

God: Nah. That isn't how I'd like you to think of Me today.

Me: How should I think of You?

God: Think of Me like the warm hand wrapped around yours as you walk right through the storm. Think of Me like the comfy wool blanket wrapped tightly around you as you face the freezing wind.

Me: I really would prefer to not to have to deal with any storms. You could just make sure that I don't have to endure any more suffering.

God: Where would the adventure be in that? If your life was without any obstacles or suffering, it wouldn't be the gift that it is. Without enduring the storms of your life you would take the sunshine for granted. I know you want Me to protect you from all suffering, but I am going to do something more important. I am going to stay with you during the storm. I will not leave you. I am the hand in yours. I am the blanket wrapped around you. I am right here.

Me: So, you won't ever be my umbrella?

God: Sometimes I will be, but not today. Today I'm something more important. Today I'm going to be something that helps you endure the cold night.

Me: What's that?

God: Your thermal underwear.

Me: That's you? You are a little too snug.

God: I told you we are tight!

There's No "If" About It

Me: Hey God.

God: Hey John.

Me: Why is my heart so closed?

God: Because you treat it like a bank vault. You gave it a knob and a combination lock.

Me: I don't want to be vulnerable.

God: To what? The world? Other people? To Me? How many graces are you going to deny yourself in the name of self-protection? I want you to be vulnerable. I want you to rely on Me. Without vulnerability there is no faith. Without being vulnerable you won't risk serving other people. Without being vulnerable you won't allow yourself to be served by others. Without vulnerability you can't share your light.

Me: But what if I get hurt?

God: There is no "if" about it. You will get hurt.

Me: Ugh.

God: Don't fret. It's all worth it. I promise. Quit thinking of your heart like a door.

Me: How should I think of my heart instead?

God: Like a big old lighthouse!

Me: What now?

God: Everyone's heart is like a giant lighthouse. It's meant for reflecting light into even the darkest ocean. Helping each other navigate the unseen shoreline. Get rid of the door. Be a lighthouse.

Me: I can't. I don't have a big enough light.

God: No worries. You can borrow Mine.

Interruption

Me: Hey God.

God: Hey John.

Me: I can't –

God: Yes, you can.

Me: You didn't let me finish what I was just about to say.

God: I didn't need to.

Signs

Me: Hey God.

God: Hey John.

Me: Can I get a sign?

God: Sure! I love signs!

Me: I need an unmistakable sign from You telling me how You want me to spend the rest of my life.

God: What are you talking about? There are signs everywhere right now.

Me: Uh, all I see are people on a bus.

God: Same thing.

Me: What is the message these alleged signs are trying to tell me?

God: Quit isolating yourself. Serve. Spread grace. Love with abandon. Forgive without hesitation. Build community. Find a way to ease the suffering of others. Get your hands messy in the business of loving your neighbor! These are my people. Treat them with care.

Me: Oh.

God: You sound disappointed.

Me: I was hoping for a bigger sign. Something like a herd of unicorns descending a rainbow to the sound of a glorious trumpet fanfare.

God: If you saw that kind of sign, it would have a completely different message for you.

Me: Which would be what?

God: To stop taking your summer cold medications after drinking red wine.

Me: Right.

God: Quit waiting for signs. Live your life. Serve others. Sow joy. You've wasted so much time waiting for a spectacular sign from Me that you haven't paid attention to the subtle whispers that are inviting you to a life of service and love.

Me: Fair enough. Can I at least get a rainbow or four-leaf clover?

God: Can't do a rainbow. How about My sign for you is letting you sit on a chewed piece of gum that somebody left on your bus seat?

Me: Uh, no thanks. I'll pass on that kind of sign.

God: Well...about that...

Me: Gross! There is gum all over my butt!

God: That's not gum. It's a sign!

Me: Of what?!?

HEY GOD. HEY JOHN.

God: My humor.
Me: Yuck...
God: I love signs!

Step Over. Step Out.

Me: Hey God.

God: Hey John.

Me: I want a bigger, more interesting life.

God: Are you sure about that?

Me: Of course.

God: Doing that would require you to step over and out of your safe little circle.

Me: What are You talking about?

God: You've drawn a small circle around your life, which has become your entire world.

Me: Huh. I guess I have.

God: Haven't you noticed that your circle is getting smaller every year? There is barely enough room for anyone but you. Don't you feel lonely in there? Isn't constantly separating yourself from others exhausting? Aren't you ready to see all that I have waiting for you?

Me: Yes! Come and rescue me!

God: Just step over and away from the walls you've built around yourself. Come join the world outside your circle. Step over. Step out.

Me: I would but I don't think I'm strong enough.

God: Of course you are. Step over. Step out.

Me: Isn't it dangerous out there? At least I know that that my circle is keeping out the bad stuff.

God: Have you ever thought that maybe the invisible lines you've drawn are doing the opposite? Maybe they are keeping the bad stuff inside the circle with you?

Me: Can't I just draw a bigger circle?

God: No more circles. No more moats. You are not an island. Quit the tyranny of invisible borders. Real freedom is waiting for you on the other side of those lines in the sand. Step over. Step out. Choose curiosity over fear. Choose adventure over comfort. Step over. Step out. Your soul is restless and it's done being caged.

Me: I think it would be easier if You would just wash the circle away for me.

God: You'd just redraw it. You need to do this yourself. Come to Me. Step over. Step out. Come into the world. Leave your terror and fretting in the circle. Step over. Step out. I'm right here. Let's get going!

Me: I can't...

God: I've made you limitless. The only confines your life will have are ones you construct yourself. Your life will only be as big as you allow it to be. Step over. Step out. I'm right here.

Me: Okay. Toes in sand. Here goes nothing...

God: Correction: Here comes everything.

Me: Stepping over...Stepping out...

God: Let's go!! Let's go!!

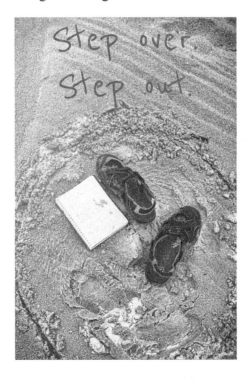

Still Work To Do

Me: Hey God.

God: Hey John.

Me: I think I'd like You to help me acquire lots of money.

God: I think you would be better off if I helped you to acquire lots of inner peace instead.

Me: I think lots of money and inner peace are the same thing.

God: I think you and I still have plenty of work to do on your heart.

Me: I think You're probably right.

It's A Journey

Me: Hey God.

God: Hey John.

Me: I wish I had as much faith in You as other people seem to.

God: Following Me isn't a competition. It's not a race to see who can reach enlightenment first. Faith is a lifelong journey through green valleys and over steep, icy mountains. Belief doesn't have a finish line and our relationship won't ever come to an end. You are on a never-ending adventure with Me into the great wild.

Me: I don't know if I'm worthy of being in a relationship with You. I have so many doubts. Everybody else seems more confident in You than I do.

God: Spirituality isn't an exclusive club only for certain people. You have as much right to talk with Me as anybody else does. I love you as much as I love any mystical guru or spiritual leader, or anyone on death row. I don't play favorites. I love every inch of you, doubts and all.

Quit comparing yourself to others. You are just as imperfectly beautiful as anybody else that I've ever created.

Me: When will my faith crisis end?

God: When you quit calling it "a faith crisis".

Me: What should I call it?

God: Your faith journey.

Me: What should I do about all my doubts?

God: Bring them along for the journey. Someday they'll make for great campfire kindling.

There's Another Word For That

Me: Hey God.

God: Hey John.

Me: I can't get my life together.

God: You're doing fine.

Me: No, I'm not. I keep falling down.

God: I wouldn't classify what you're doing as "falling".

Me: What would You call it?

God: Bouncing.

About Every 156 Seconds

Me: Hey God.

God: Hey John.

Me: Heal my heart.

God: I'd love to. Just give it to Me.

Me: Uh. I'm not ready for that step yet.

God: Well, that will make helping you kind of tricky.

Me: Fine. I'll find something else to fix my heart.

God: Alrighty.

156 SECONDS LATER

Me: Heal my heart.

God: I'd love to. Just give it to Me.

Me: Uh. I'm not ready –

God: It's gonna be one of those days, huh?

Me: Yup.

Aliens

Me: Hey God.

God: Hey John.

Me: I'm worried about my future.

God: Oh, because of the alien invasion?

Me: Huh?

God: Oops. Never mind.

Me: What alien invasion??!

God: Exactly. Forget I said anything.

Me: I'm freaking out!

God: You really shouldn't. I was thinking of a different planet. You guys are totally fine.

Me: Wait. I know what you're doing. You are just trying to remind me to quit worrying about a future that I can't control and to focus more of my attention on the present moment. You want me to keep my eyes and heart on what is happening around me right now and not to fret over an imagined future problem.

God: Exactly!

Me: You're teaching me that my anxiety only has as much power over me as I allow it. The enemy of my anxiety is the copious amounts of loving attention that I give to the present moment. You want me to know that worrying about the unknown future is nothing more than wasted energy.

God: That sounds exactly like something I would want you to know.

Me: Alien invasion?! How ridiculous!

God: Super ridiculous.

Me: You had me going for a second.

God: Uh huh.

Me: Well, I'm going to go grocery shopping. I'll talk to You later.

God: Okay. Make sure you get a few of pallets of bottled water and a couple hundred boxes of ramen noodles. Also, is there any chance you can buy a ham radio in the next day or so?

Me: Why?!

God: You know...just in case.

Me:

God:

Me: Not funny.

God: Heh.

Worthy Of Love

Me: Hey God.

God: Hey John.

Me: I'm ready for my life to take off! I'm tired of waiting. Let's get going! I'm ready to live a life that I love!

God: Awesome. Before we get started, I need you to answer one quick question.

Me: Sure!

God: Do you love yourself?

Me: I love my family.

God: That's not what I asked.

Me: I do my best to love other people, even those who get under my skin.

God: Uh huh. But do you love yourself?

Me: I'm not sure what that has to do with –

God: It has everything to do with it. How can you have a life that you love if you don't love yourself? How can you love other people if you haven't found a way to fall in love with the person that you are? How can you show kindness and generosity to everyone else if you don't extend those same things to yourself? How do you forgive others if you won't forgive yourself?

Me: But I'm a mess. I'm a failure. I'm so flawed. I'm weak. I'm –

God: Hush.

Me:

God: You are My artwork. You are worthy of happiness. You are worthy of abundance. You are worthy of joy. You are worthy of forgiveness. You are worthy of every little drop of light and goodness that exists in the universe that I've created for you. You are worthy of love.

Me: Yeah, but –

God: You are worthy of love.

Me: Maybe, however I am –

God: You are worthy of love.

Me: I don't know. I have –

God: You are worthy of love. Say it.

Me: I'm worthy...of love...

God: That wasn't very sincere. Try again.

Me: I'm worthy of love...

God: Now, tell yourself that you're in love with who you are.

Me: I can't. Not yet, at least.

God: You will. Everything will change when you do.

Me: I just want my life to have a purpose.

God: It does. Your purpose is to love and serve people.

Me: Okay…

God: Starting with yourself.

Me: Yuck.

God: Be my instrument. Love yourself in the unconditional way that I love you.

Me: I don't know...

God: Let's keep trying.

Me: Fine...

God: You are worthy of love.

Me: I am worthy of love.

God: Say it again. You are worthy of love.

Me: I am worthy of love.

God: Say it again. Say it again. Say it again and again and again and again and again and again and again and again.

Worthy Of Love II

We are worthy of love.

We are worthy of happiness.

Joy isn't a rare flower; joy is everywhere.

And we are worthy of it.

Joy blooms even during the winter of suffering.

We are worthy of love.

We are loved.

You are worthy of love.

You are.

You were born this way.

ME: Hey God.
God: Hey John
ME: Help me change
God: Nope.
ME: Why not?
God: Because you
haven't tried
being who you
were born to be
yet.

ME: Who is that?

God: Loved

Plans

Me: Hey God.

God: Hey John.

Me: I know just how I want my day to go! I have an airtight plan!

God: Challenge accepted.

Me: What?

God: Nothing...

It's Hard To Hold Hands
With A Fist

I have never shared any of my other writing here on this page because I view this as sacred space. I like to keep things here very simple. However... I'm breaking that rule (just for today) because I've gotten a few messages from folks who read a piece that I wrote a few weeks ago and thought I should post it here in case anybody needs to read it. Grief and loss (especially around the holidays) are the most trying of situations that we can face as people of faith. The experience of watching a loved one pass away is the ultimate human experience and the following is an entry that I wrote in reflection of being at my mother's side when she fell into God's hands five years ago. I hope this helps somebody out there who is hurting today.

God Bless – John Roedel

* * * * *

"I hate. I hate. I hate," my mom chanted unconsciously on her deathbed.

"It's going to be okay. Everything is going to be okay," I lied softly to her while holding her cold, clenched fist in my hand.

With her eyes pinched shut she responded with another round of, "I hate. I hate. I hate."

It had been five days since she had said anything other than "I hate" and it was breaking my heart. The "I hates" always came in threes. I spent hours by her bedside trying to figure out why. I had considered for a while that she was trying to communicate with me through some sort of metaphysical code. Perhaps she was telling me to make sure to water her plants three times a day? I made a couple dozen "I hate" anagrams trying to solve the mystery.

Eat Hi – A referendum against small talk we both disputed?

Ha Tie – A joke between us because I never tied my shoes and she was certain that someday I'd trip in a super embarrassing situation?

The IA – Did she want me to take her to Iowa?

Eventually, it became clear that there was no hidden message in what she was saying. The endless stream of socially awkward neurologists made it known to us that whatever my mom was saying was probably just her brain misfiring due to the trauma of the collecting pressure of blood that was building on it.

"I hate. I hate. I hate."

I didn't want those to be the last words that she would utter before the unstoppable bleeding in her brain would finally claim her life. I was desperate for her to say anything else.

"It is going to be okay. You are loved. You are looooovveed. Loooved." I said, like a parent trying to get their baby say their first word.

Although I am prone to abject selfishness and can easily make most things about me, I was pretty sure that her litany of I hates didn't have much to do with me. If I had to guess, I'm pretty sure she was just commenting on how much she hated her current situation. My mom abhorred doctors and people fussing over her and here she was enduring both horrors at once.

I remember trying to hold her hand, but it was always clenched too tight, so I settled for just resting mine on top hers while watching her fade away.

I sat by her for another three days in that grim little hospital room, witnessing her grapple with death. I imagined during that time that they were tied up in some pretty heated negotiations.

Death: Alright, let's go.

My Mom: Shut up.

Death: Please?

My Mom: Bite me.

Death: I'll go make some coffee.

My Mom: Make a double pot. You're gonna be here a while.

Death: Great...

Eventually my mom was moved to a much more comfortable hospice center for her last couple of days on Earth. There were no more mechanical whirls or beeps from monitors that plagued our days together in the old hospital room. At the hospice there was only the sound of quiet dignity of my mom's final few thousand breaths. It was so much more relaxed and reverent there. But there was one familiar sound that followed us to the hospice:

"I hate. I hate. I hate," she continued.

"It's going to be okay," I responded on cue. My hand around her fist.

A young hospice nurse walked in and took a look at the two of us. We were quite a pair. My mom fading away and me looking like I hadn't showered since the late 90s.

"Hold her hand," the nurse instructed kindly but firmly. That's a difficult balance in tone to manage, but she did it.

I tried to explain that my mom wasn't going to allow for that. Her hand was too tightly coiled. The nurse shook her head like a fastball pitcher who had just been given the sign to throw a changeup. She walked over and took my mom's fisted hand, gently turned it over and began to tenderly massage the base of her palm. Within a second or two her fist opened up like a spring flower and I was able to lace my fingers with hers.

This was the first time we had held hands in over 25 years. Everything melted away. The room.

The lovely hospice nurse. It was just my mom and me. A mother and her son having one last walk together through the universe. Two souls parting. Saying everything that needed to be said. When I regained my senses I saw the nurse on the other side of my mom's bed holding her opposite hand.

She smiled at me:

"It's hard to hold hands with a fist," the nurse said in the softest of voices.

I nodded in agreement. I was crying. It was the first time that I had broken down during my mom's six-week battle.

"It's going to be okay. You are loved," I whispered to my mom.

"Okay..." she whispered in reply.

She never spoke again.

A day later my mom passed away surrounded by family and with her hands being held. She ventured across the veil and into God's arms while feeling a pulse beat against her still body.

"Okay" was her last word.

Perfect.

Every day I
Try my
Best to
Remember the
Final lesson
My mom
Taught me:
Live with
Open hands
And not
Clenched fists.
Okay.
I will.
I will.
Okay.

Unstoppable

Me: Hey God.

God: Hey John.

Me: Why did you allow my son to have autism?

God: Because I knew that he could carry it on his shoulders. I knew he would show the world that a soul doesn't have a blueprint. He will demonstrate that the miracle of life comes in all shapes, sizes and forms. Your son is here to remind everyone and especially you – that grief can't outrun joy and, most importantly, to provide an example to all that LOVE IS UNSTOPPABLE!

Me: What are you talking about?

God: Love always wins. It's a fixed game. Love can be labeled as "different" but love keeps trucking toward. Love doesn't care about what any diagnosis says about it. Love breaks through chains. Love survives. Love finds a way. Love is the ultimate life hack.

Me: Those are nice words but I just want him not to have to struggle anymore.

God: Every beam of sunlight struggles to find its way through a piece of stained glass, and when that shard of light finally pierces the thick painted glass, it transforms everything around it. That glow illuminates every corner of a dark room with a rainbow of colors. Your child's autism is just a barrier for his light to shine through and when it does...

Me: It's love?

God: Amen. The light might be in a different shade or shape than you were expecting, but don't mistake it. His unique light is pure and radiant love. If you want proof of My existence, just watch the light show playing out right in front of you.

Me: Are you sure he is going to be okay?

God: He's going to be better than okay. He's going to be...

Me: Unstoppable.

My Favorite Cause

Me: Hey God.

God: Hey John.

Me: I just even can't handle life today.

God: Sure, you can. Don't worry. You've got this.

Me: I don't think so.. I'm a mess. I feel like my back is against the wall.

God: That's not a wall.

Me: It's not?

God: Nope, it's Me. Don't worry. We've got this.

Me: I'm such a lost cause.

God: Those are my favorite kind of causes. Don't worry. I've got this.

Me: Alright; I'll get out of bed...

God: Let's go! Let's go! Let's go! Beauty awaits!

Hey John

One small Kindness

Can become an

infinite ripple

Love,
God

Breathe In. Breathe Out.

Me: Hey God.

God: Hey John.

Me: Anxiety stinks. I was up all night tossing and turning.

God: Yeah, you seem a little rough around the edges today.

Me: Is it really that obvious? I thought I was hiding it well.

God: Well, you kind of have the look of a convenience store hot dog that has been in the warmer for six days.

Me: That's exactly how I feel! I miss being a child. I had so much less to worry about back then. I was more carefree and connected to life.

God: You can have that again.

Me: I don't think so. I'm constantly tired from being afraid all the time.

God: You shouldn't allow fear to have such a hold on you.

Me: I know, but even right now I can't escape this feeling of dread. It's like I have a heavy barbell on my chest and makes it hard to think about or do anything else.

God: Just focus on your next breath. There is nothing you can do about what will happen to you ten minutes from now, but you can control this moment. Take in a deep breath. Hold it. Let it out. When you feel helpless, just take ownership of the air passing through your lungs and remember that you are alive. Breathe in. Breathe out. You're alive. Breathe in. Breathe out. You're alive.

Me: Easier said than done. My anxiety is overwhelming. And it's so frustrating that I don't exactly know what it is that I'm afraid of. It's like I'm constantly living in a scene from a horror movie where the scary music builds and builds, but no monster ever jumps out to eat me. I'm in a perpetual state of terror over a destruction that never comes. I'm living under an invisible knife that I'm certain is always about to fall on me.

God: Quit believing in the lies that fear tells. Fear wants you all to itself. Fear desires nothing more than you paralyzed in bed. Fear has trained your brain to function in a constant state of worry about "What will happen to me tomorrow?" instead of concerning yourself with "What is happening to me right now?"

Me: Can't you just cure my anxiety?

God: I have a better idea. I know how you can get rid of it yourself. You can defeat fear by not allowing it to access your imagination. I gave mankind an incredible facility for creativity. But creativity is a double-edged sword because it can be used to change the world for the better, and it can also make a prison for yourself or others. You keep letting fear draw and drink from your well of imagination. When you allow that, fear comes up with new and inventive ways to terrify you. When you were a child, your imagination wove blankets of promise and limitless possibilities. What happened to that kid?

Me: I guess I grew up...

God: Don't confuse GROWING UP with GIVING UP! What would your life look like if you cut fear off from your imagination and only granted your dreams access to it? Can you picture a life where you starve your anxieties and only feed your hope? Can you envision leading a life guided by purpose instead of a list of imaginary fears? Imagine how it would be if you used your creativity to dream up possibilities instead of nightmares.

Me: That would be nice.

God: You can have all of that again. I gave you an imagination to play and to create, not to fret. To create, not to destroy. To paint angels, not to invent demons. Whenever you feel the dread of anxiety wash over you, just remember:

Breathe in.
Breathe out.
You're alive.
And then always remember who you are.

Me: Who is that?

God: My child.

Retirement Plan

Me: Hey God.

God: Hey John.

Me: I need a job.

God: Perfect timing. I have a great opportunity for you.

Me: Sweet! What is it?

God: I need someone to demonstrate the power of mercy. To show the value of compassion over social status. The ideal candidate would have to be proficient in forgiveness. They would also need to be prone to choosing kindness instead of needing to win an argument.

Me: Huh. Sounds complicated.

God: It really isn't.

Me: What does it pay?

God: Nothing, but you should see the retirement plan I'm offering.

Rejection

Me: Hey God.

God: Hey John.

Me: I give up.

God: How come?

Me: Because I keep getting rejected. I'm tired of failure.

Emily Dickinson: So was I.

Abraham Lincoln: So was I.

Walt Disney: So was I.

JK Rowling: So was I.

Babe Ruth: So was I.

Albert Einstein: So was I.

Van Gogh: So was I.

Henry Ford: So was I.

Saint Peter: So was I.

Dr. Seuss: So was I.

Oprah Winfrey: So was I.

Thomas Edison: So was I.

Jim Carey: So was I.

Lucille Ball: So was I.

Michael Jordan: So was -

Me: Okay. Okay. I get the point.

God: Great! Don't give up. The plant never knows how deep the soil is until it finally emerges into the light. Right. Now, can you all please let me finish my shower in peace? This is all a little weird.

Henry Ford: Make sure you use conditioner. Your hair has looked a bit wild lately.

Thomas Edison: I was thinking that same thing!

Unseen

Me: Hey God.

God: Hey John.

Me: I don't think You're real.

God: Are you sure about that?

Me: No...

God: I'm right here.

Me: But You're so unseen.

God: That's because you're so unlooking.

Me: Unlooking? That's not a real word.

God: Are you sure about that?

Me: No...

God: Things can be real even if you don't fully believe or understand them. You may not be searching for Me, but that doesn't mean that I'm not real. The thing is, I won't ever be real for you if you keep looking through tiny keyholes to find Me. Quit straining your eyes. Open the door. I'm right out here. Leave your room. I may not be what you expect, but I'm real. I'm realer than any fear or doubt you've ever had.

Me: Having faith is hard.

God: It's supposed to be hard. Faith takes courage. To seek the unseen is tricky. That's why it's not called "certainty." Take a risk by leaving your room to follow the breadcrumb path of miracles that I've laid out. Stop looking through keyholes and open the door. Leave your room. You have the courage to come and find Me.

Me: I can't. My courage isn't real.

God: Are you sure about that?

Me: No...

God: Just because you don't believe in something doesn't mean that it's not real.

Me: Fine. I'm coming to find You.

God: I won't be hard to see. Just stop unlooking.

Me: Is unlooking really a word?

God: Come outside and I promise that it won't be any more.

Edited

Me: Hey God.

God: Hey John.

Me: You never answer any of my prayers!

Me: Everybody else has more than I do!!

Me: I deserve more! Give it to me!!!

Me: I'm already blessed.

God: There ya go.

Purpose

Me: Hey God.

God: Hey John.

Me: My life has no purpose.

God: Stop talking. It's my turn.

Me: Uh? Whoa. I don't think You're allowed to –

God: Welcome to Tough Love Monday. You don't think your life has a purpose? Have you ever considered that simply embracing the fact that you are alive IS your purpose? Are you living the life you want right now? Or are you just passing time waiting for something to happen for you?

Me: Well, I was just hoping You would tell me what it is You want me to do with my life.

God: Well, first, I want you to go out and live it. You act like you are serving time in a prison cell, hoping that one day your sentence will be commuted by Me and you'll be released to start living a fuller life. There is no jail. Your time being physically alive is finite. It's like an ice cube melting in your hand. Quit wasting it. The clock is ticking.

Me: I think I could if You just showed me a miracle or something to inspire me.

God: Your life IS the miracle. All life is. You're waiting for an "ah-ha" moment? That already happened on the day that you were born. I did the hard part by forming you out of the void of nothingness. What have you done to honor that miracle? You want your life to have purpose? Your life is the purpose! Get off your duff and live. Life is precious. Don't waste it.

Me: I'll try.

Good: Oh, and wax your unibrow. It's scaring the neighborhood children.

Me: I don't like Tough Love Monday.

God: Nobody does.

Holes

Me: Hey God.

God: Hey John.

Me: I feel terrible today. This must be the low point of my life.

God: That depends.

Me: On what?

God: On how deep a hole you want to keep digging for yourself.

Me: Oh. I was wondering how I got down here.

God: Put down that shovel and climb up and out of there. I have something beautiful that I want to show you.

Me: What's that?

God: Mercy.

Dang

Me: Hey God.

God: Hey John.

Me: Today is going to be an amazing day!

God: It's always going to be an amazing day!

Me: I'm ready to take a huge risk!

God: Wonderful!

Me: It's going to be a little scary but I am going to be brave!

God: Go get it!

Me: Here we go!

Anxiety: Hey John.

Me: Dang. Dang. Dang.

Anxiety: What?

Me: What are you doing here? I was just leaving.

Anxiety: Well, once I heard that you were taking a huge risk I knew that I had to give you some advice before you walked out the door.

Me: What's your advice?

Anxiety: Don't do it. You're sure to fail.

Me: You don't even know what it is that I am going to do!

Anxiety: I don't need to. Whatever it is that you are planning on doing will blow up in your face.

Me: Dang. Dang. Dang.

Anxiety: I just want you to avoid the inevitable disappointment coming your way. Accept who you are and quit setting yourself up for failure. Put down those car keys and let's just hang out at home.

Me: I just really wanted to try.

Anxiety: I know, but it's pointless. Look, I'll go grab your pajamas and bring back a package of Oreos for you to binge on. It will be safer. I'll be right back. Just wait here.

Me: Ugh. I can't believe Anxiety showed up. This is a horrible development.

God: I disagree.. It's a really good sign.

Me: Of what??!

God: Anxiety usually shows up right before a person is about to do something remarkable. It is afraid that it's losing control over you. Anxiety is getting desperate. The closer you get to your dreams, the more internal resistance you can expect to face. It's a great sign.

Me: I never thought of it like that.

God: Want to get going?

Me: You bet! It's going to be an amazing day!

God: It's always going to be an amazing day!

Me: Let's go!

Anxiety: Hey John, I'm back. I couldn't find any Oreos, but I did find some stale marshmallows in the back of your pantry. They should do the trick. Do you still have that membership to Netflix?

Anxiety: Uh, John?

Anxiety: John? Johnny? Buddy? Pal? Are you still here?

Anxiety: John??!!!

Anxiety: Dang. Dang. Dang.

Zzzzzz...

Me: Hey God.

God: Hey John.

Me: Insomnia again...

God: That's because you're angry at somebody. You need to let it go. Forgive them.

Me: No. I can't. I won't. Never.

God: You should.

Me: I'm too angry at them. I've been hurt so deeply. I want revenge.

God: The best revenge is to forgive completely. It releases all control that person has over you. You can finally be free to move on. Grudges and resentments are the burglars of joy. Let go of the pain, you don't need it any longer. Anger doesn't serve you in the long run. It's a short-term fix.

Me: I don't want to let them off so easily by forgiving them.

God: You aren't. By forgiving them you are letting YOURSELF off easy.

Me: I'm so tired.

God: Forgive. Let it go. Holding on to your anger is hard work. Forgive and you'll find rest. Trust me.

Me: I'll try but I don't think it... Zzzzzzzzz.

God: Nice work.

Me: Zzzzzzzzz.

God: G'night Johnny-Boy.

Stillness

Me: Hey God.

God: Hey John.

Me: Yeesh.

God: What's up?

Me: I've got a lot on my mind.

God: I have an idea. You should spend some time in quiet reflection this morning.

Me: Huh. Maybe.

God: Seriously. Just close your eyes and rest in the comforting stillness of My presence.

Me: Okay...sure.

God: Go ahead and get started.

Me:

God:

Me:

God:

Me:

God:

Me: Mmmmm.

God: What?

Me: Tacos.

God: Empty your mind of all thoughts and embrace the silence.

Me: Of course.

God:

Me:

God:

Me: Mmmmm.

God: Shhh.

Me:

God:

Me:

God:

Me: Mmmm.

God: Don't dwell on any one thought. Allow the peace of quiet reflection fill – wait a second, are you drooling?!

Me: Probably.

God: Ew. Why?

Me: Tacos.

God: I think we're done here.

Barely

Me: Hey God.

God: Hey John.

Me: It's over. I'm beaten. Depression has won.

God: That's not true. You won.

Me: How can You tell?

God: Because you're still here.

Me: Barely.

God: Barely is all it takes. Barely is amazing. Barely is a miracle. With every single heartbeat you are teaching depression that it can't win and reminding it that hope will triumph over the darkness. The breath you are drawing right now is your victory parade. You have won because you're still alive. You are still here. You are still here. Barely or not, you are still here. Say that out loud.

Me: I am still here.

God: And so am I. You aren't alone. Who is winning?

Me: I am. I am still here.

God: Of course, you are. You are stronger than you know.

Depression: This is getting super awkward. I think I'm going to take the day off.

God: Good idea.

Pain Vs. Pane

Me: Hey God.

God: Hey John.

Me: My world has gotten so small.

God: That's because you are looking out at it through a tiny window. You have no idea what you are missing. The world is an amazing place.

Me: Are you saying that I need a bigger window?

God: No. You don't need a bigger window. You just need to jump through the dang thing. Quit looking out at the world and become a part of it. Join the party.

Me: Wait – what? You want me to jump through the window?

God: Yep, like a boss. Crash through it like a stunt man.

Me: Won't that hurt?

God: Yes. It will be a little pane-full.

Me:

God: Heh.

Me:

God: Get it? Panefull?

Me:

God: Panefull?

Me: Ugh.

God: Because it's a window. Pane? Heh. Get it?

Me: I got it...

God: I'm hilarious. Now get out there and live your life. Jump through that window. Explore the splendor. Quit worrying about being safe and go get some mud in your toes. Befriend the unknown.

Me: I'll try.

God: You really didn't like my window joke?

Me: No.

God: How come?

Me: Because I saw right through it.

God:

Me: Get it?

God: I got it...

Me: Heh.

God: We better hold off on our comedy tour.

And Again...

Me: Hey God.

God: Hey John.

Me: Take away my sadness and fear.

God: Sure. Just go ahead and hand those two over to Me. I'll get rid of them.

Me: No.

God: Just let go.

Me: No.

God: I thought you wanted Me to lift the burden of fear and sadness from your heart.

Me: I really do. I'm exhausted.

God: Okay. Then give them to Me.

Me: No. I don't know who I'd be without them.

God: I do.

Me: Who?

God: You'd be free...

Me: That sounds wonderful. I can't go on like this.

God: What do you say? Want to try again?

Me: Yes.

God: Great! Ask Me again.

Me: Take away my sadness and fear.

God: Hand them over. Let go.

Me: No.

God: John...

Me: I'm sorry.

God: Don't be. I'm not giving up on you. We're in this together.

Me: Can we try again?

God: And again and again and again and again and...

9/11/2016

Me: Hey God.

God: Hey John.

Me: I can still remember how terrified I was 15 years ago today. The world felt upside down. I was angry. I wanted revenge against the people who had carried out such a violent attack. I felt bloodthirsty.

God: What good will getting revenge do to your heart? Revenge is a hunger that is never satisfied. Instead of striking back, choose to sow love and understanding instead of intolerance. Don't stoke the fires of rage and violence in the world. Striving for peace isn't a sign of weakness, it's sign of strength. It takes courage to fight the evils of the world with a hopeful heart. Peace will come.

Me: The world is in such a horrible mess.

God: Someday wars will end. The wheel of violence will stop spinning. I have faith in mankind. The world will change and evil will dissipate.

Me: How? I don't see a way.

God: Peace is the way.

Me: Lord, make me an instrument of Your peace. Where there is hatred, let me sow love; where there is injury, pardon; where there is doubt, faith; where there is despair, hope; where there is darkness, light; where there is sadness, joy.

God: Amen. You must be the change that you wish to see in the world.

Which One?

Me: Hey God.

God: Hey John.

Me: Ugh. A part of me thinks that today is going to be horrible. Filled with nothing but worry, conflict and loneliness. That this will be the day when I finally give up.

God: Okay.

Me: But then there is another part of me that thinks that today is going to be amazing. It's going to be one of those moments that I look back on one day as the day I finally started living again. Embracing possibility. Following my dreams. Believing in my purpose. A transformative day.

God: Okay.

Me: Well??

God: Well what?

Me: Which one of those days are You going to let happen?

God: That's funny. I was about to ask you that exact question.

Significant

Me: Hey God.

God: Hey John.

Me: I'm insignificant.

God: I don't create anything insignificant. I had to make you. I had no choice.

Me: Why?

God: Because this infinite and complex universe wouldn't have been the same without you.

Me: My life is that important?

God: All life is that important. No life is insignificant. Every life is a gift. Don't squander yours.

Me: How can I avoid that?

God: By living significantly.

Ghosts

Me: Hey God.

God: Hey John.

Me: Are ghosts real?

God: The ones haunting your heart are. The phantoms of your heart are the ones banging the walls and wailing at night when you are trying to sleep.

Me: Yikes!

God: These spirits are the echoes of guilt and they won't quit until you forgive yourself. Don't let your past haunt you any longer. Stop giving your old regrets permission to occupy your heart. Release the ghosts of your mistakes. Stop allowing your heart to be a haunted house for all the things that you believe you've done wrong. Forgive yourself. Ask for forgiveness. Ghosts hate reconciliation and tranquility. Asking mercy is like throwing back the curtains at daybreak. The light of absolution will wash away any spirit.

JOHN ROEDEL

Me: What if I'm beyond forgiving? I'm not sure that I can forgive myself.

God: Of course, you can.

Me: What makes You say that?

God: Because I've already done it. Let the light in. Open the shutters.

Me: I'm scared...but I'll try.

God: You ain't afraid of no ghosts!

Anxiety Hack

Me: Hey God.

God: Hey John.

Me: Good morning...

God: Great morning! Time to get moving! There is so much waiting for you out there! Let's go! Let's go!

Me: I can't. My anxiety won't let me get out of bed today.

God: There's an easy way around that problem.

Me: What is it?

God: Quit asking it for permission.

Me: Ah snap.

God: Let's go! Let's go! Miracles await!

Act IV:
Show me something
beautiful.

Surrendering to what is happening to me.
The more vulnerability I allow myself to reveal
to God, the deeper our conversations become.
I pour my heart out onto the page.
I feel connected to something beyond me.
Who is this person that I am becoming? God says
that I am not changing but that I am finally
accepting who I was meant to be all along.
Having a relationship with God
is dangerous work.
God is thawing me.
God is inviting me back into the world.
God is ready to show me something beautiful.
I'm surrendering to it all.

I pray because I can't help myself. I pray because I'm helpless. I pray because the need flows out of me all the time – waking and sleeping. It doesn't change God – it changes me.
—C.S. Lewis

The Courage Of A Little Leaf

Me: Hey God.

God: Hey John.

Me: I can't believe it's already Fall!

God: I love the colors. Leaves falling like rain. The way the orange sunset lingers against the cooling blue sky. Everything is transforming! Welcome to this season of change!

Me: When will I change?

God: When you finally show the courage of a little leaf.

Me: Uh, what?

God: Die to who you were. Change your colors. Let go of your tired way of living. Break from your branch. Have the faith to flutter away from safety. Fall into what will come next for you. Don't hang on to your old self anymore. Snap. Be like a September leaf. Embrace transformation.

Me: I'm afraid.

God: Good. That means something amazing is about to happen.

Me: Eek.

God: Fall, baby, Fall.

ME: Hey God

God: Hey John.

ME: Help me to become kind. of a big deal.

God: I'd love to!

Flipped

Me: Hey God.

God: Hey John.

Me: Do you love me?

God: Of course.

Me: Good. Now prove it, please. Take away all my problems and make my life easy.

God: Nope.

Me: Why not?

God: Because I love you.

Me: Ugh. You keep flipping things around on me.

God: It's called spiritual judo.

Me: Why can't You just take away of my problems?

God: Do you want to have an easy life where everything is handed to you on a plate, but ultimately on your deathbed you will feel cheated? Or do you want to live a meaningful life where you prevail through suffering and overcome countless obstacles, finally to find your purpose? You can't have both.

Me: I guess I want a meaningful life.
God: Good. Now prove it, please.
Me: Whoa.
God: Flipped!

Huge Hands

Me: Hey God.

God: Hey John.

Me: People keep telling me that You only give us what we can handle?

God: I've heard that expression too. It's sort of reassuring, isn't it?

Me: Yeah, but I can't handle very much. I think I'm already at my limit.

God: You're not even close.

Me: Um, so, I should be expecting more burdens?

God: You bet.

Me: Great... Look, God, I've got super small hands. Like Oompa Loompa-sized hands. I should feature in a circus act. Objects appear three times larger than they are when I'm holding them. I have the glove size of a Hobbit. Even Donald Trump makes fun of my hands. Come on...I don't think I can carry any more than I already am. My hands are full and I'm going to start dropping stuff soon.

God: Relax. You'll be fine.

Me: Well, what about the whole thing where You are only giving us as much as we can handle??

God: In your case I'm only going to give you as much as the TWO OF US can handle together. Hint: It's going to be a lot!

Me: Ugh.

God: Don't worry.

Me: Why shouldn't I?

God: I have huge hands.

Me: Alright...

God: You aren't alone. I'm right here. Give Me something to carry.

Me: I don't want to.

God: That's the real issue. You don't want to give up what is causing you pain.

Me: They're mine. I don't know who I would be without my sorrows.

God: Quit being selfish with your suffering. Let Me have it.

Me: But there is so much...

God: I brought a wheelbarrow.

Terrible Roommate

Me: Hey God.

Doubt: Hey John.

Me: Barf. What are you doing here?

Doubt: I'm always here. I'm like your roommate. By the way, it's your turn to do the dishes. Seriously, there's something funky happening in the sink right now.

Me: I'd like some privacy. I'm trying to talk with God.

Doubt: Cool. Say "hi" for me.

Me: Wait – I didn't think that you believed in God?

Doubt: Oh, I totally believe that God exists now. I've evolved my thinking on the whole thing.

Me: Great!

Doubt: I just don't think that God listens to anything you have to say.

Me: Oh...that's not so great.

Doubt: Have any of your prayers ever been answered?

Me: Yes.

Doubt: Which ones? Did God heal your parents on their deathbed after you begged Him to? Did God cure your son's autism? I remember how many nights you tearfully pleaded for that to happen. Did God take away any of those heartaches from you?

Me: No...

Doubt: What about the thousands of times you have asked for God to take away your crushing depression and anxiety? God hasn't done anything about that, right?

Me: Right.

Doubt: Face it, dude. God just isn't ever going to answer any of your prayers.

Me: Maybe not.

Doubt: Why bother then? At best it appears that God is just too busy to hear your cries for help, and at worst, it would seem like God just doesn't care about how much you suffer. God just ain't listening.

Me: I disagree.

Doubt: Do you? When was the last time you asked God to take away something that is causing you heartache or pain?

Me: I'm not sure. It's been a while.

Doubt: That means that you have finally given up on this whole prayer experiment of yours. Which makes me pretty happy.

Me: No. It just means that I'm starting to finally figure out that there is a reason for my suffering. There is purpose to it. If I had never had to face any struggles, I wouldn't know how strong that I really am. Every fall I have had has taught me amazing life lessons. If God were to have taken away all the things that broke my heart, I wouldn't be the person I am today.

Doubt: But God is allowing you to suffer!

Me: No – God is allowing me to grow, to find courage and to overcome hardship. If I never knew what pain was then I wouldn't have ever come to know the power of perseverance.

Doubt: So, it sounds like to me that you are okay with God testing you.

Me: This isn't a test. It's life. It's messy, beautiful, painful, chaotic, joyful – all at the same time. I'm not here to float gently through it. I'm here to leave my mark. To succeed. To fail. To grieve and to dance. It's all meant to be an adventure.

Doubt: I hate adventures. How can you be sure that God isn't just leaving you to twist in the wind on your own?

Me: I can't be 100 % sure – but that's why it's called "faith" and not "certainty."

Doubt: Whatever.

Me: These days I've changed the things I ask God for. I don't ask for the bad things to be taken away; I ask for the courage to remain hopeful in the face of whatever storm I'm facing.

Doubt: God doesn't care what happens to you. Trust me. You need to start seeing this whole thing my way soon before it's too late.

Me: I'd rather be wrong about God than be right about you.

Doubt: You are a chump.

Me: I don't think so.

God: Neither do I.

Me: Hey God.

God: Hey John.

Me: When did You get here?

God: I've been here the whole time. I'm like your roommate. By the way you should get on those dishes. They are stacking up. You have a bowl in your sink that is about to become sentient.

Me: Doubt and I have just been arguing about Your nature.

God: I know. I heard everything.

Me: Why didn't You chime in?

God: I didn't need to. You summed it up quite nicely.

Me: Sweet! Maybe there is some hope for me yet.

God: Totally.

Doubt: I feel like I'm a third wheel.

Me: Now that you mention it…

Come Out!

Me: Hey God.

God: Hey John.

Me: I know we had a plan to do stuff but I can't. I'm not leaving my house today.

God: How come?

Me: I'm too afraid.

God: Of what?

Me: Everything.

God: Be more specific if you can.

Me: I guess that I'm afraid of all the darkness that exists in the world.

God: Nope. That's not it. You aren't afraid of the dark. You have learned to prefer the shadows. You are afraid of something else.

Me: What's that?

God: You're afraid of the light.

Me: That doesn't any sense. Why would I be afraid of that?!

God: Because you don't feel worthy of it. You don't think you deserve good things to happen to you. You have wrongly convinced yourself that the darkness is all you deserve.

Me: Alright that's enough. I'm done talking for today. Goodbye.

God: You are worthy of every ray of light that exists. Go find it. Bathe in it.

Me: I said goodbye.

God: You are worthy of love. You are worthy of grace. You are worthy of all the goodness of the world. You are worthy of starting your life over. You're worthy of letting go of who you were. You are worthy of the light.

Me: Stop it!

God: Quit listening to the monsters under your bed that have convinced you that you aren't deserving. They want you to cower with them. You won't. You deserve the light. Come out.

Me: No. Leave me alone.

God: Come out. I love you.

Me: I'm going to get angry if You keep -

God: You're worthy of happiness. You deserve good things. I promise. I love you. Come out. It's all waiting for you. Come out. I love you.

Me: But I'm so used to the dark.

God: It's okay. I've got sunglasses for you. Come out.

Me: I'm terrified.

God: Good. That means a grand adventure awaits.

Me: So bright...

God: Don't fret. I love you. Come out. Come out.

Right Now

Me: Hey God.

God: Hey John.

Me: I've been stuck in the same place for years.

God: Yep.

Me: Why won't things change for me?

God: Because you have become used to life in a cocoon. You keep saying that you are going to burst out soon, but it never happens.

Me: Yeah – here's the thing – it's nice and safe in here.

God: Safety is overrated. Nobody ever changed the world by being safe. Life spent in safety is like wasting a beautiful beach day by sitting locked up in your car. I didn't labor over every inch of your creation for you to seek nothing but comfort. I made you to join the chaotic swirl of joy and heartbreak that is waiting for you outside your cocoon. Want to change your life? Quit talking and go do it. A butterfly doesn't get its wings by making heartfelt promises to transform. They just do it. Get moving!

Me: Fine. I'll change. First, you should take away all my fears. Then I should be good to go.

God: Why would I do that?

Me: Because fear sucks.

God: You must be using it all wrong. Fear is one of the best gifts that I've ever given you. You're welcome by the way.

Me: What?? I'm not thanking you for that! Fear is the monster preventing me from being the person that I want to be.

God: Nope. Fear isn't a rope that binds you or prevents you from being free. There is no rope. There are only choices. And right now you are choosing to not move, or grow, or change. Allow your fear to help you.

Me: How exactly does fear help me?

God: By telling you that you are on the right path. Life is meant to be challenging and change is scary. Giving up on your ego is terrifying. Serving others can be frightening. There is nothing scarier than trusting in Me and following your dreams. Fear is there to tell you to keep kicking and clawing at the cocoon wall, because once it breaks open and the light pours in, everything in your life will transform. Everything you want is just on the other side.

Me: But -

God: No more excuses, fear is not responsible for all your problems. It's time to ask the tough question: Do you really want to change? Are you ready to leave the cocoon?

Me: Yes...

God: Prove it. Give the cocoon wall a solid kick and then you'll finally see.

Me: See what?

God: Your wings.

Breaking Down. Breaking Dawn.

Me: Hey God.

God: Hey John.

Me: I'm coming apart.

God: Hold on.

Me: I can't. I just can't.

God: Yes, you can. Unclench your jaw. Find a beautiful thought in your mind and focus on it. Breathe deeply. In. Out. In. Out. Hold on. Don't let go. Shadows are passing. Hold on. Light is coming.

Me: You don't understand. I'm breaking down.

God: And I'm The Breaking Dawn. Light is here. Light is here. Light is here. Colors are back. Magnificent colors are everywhere. Light is here. Darkness loses again. Light is here.

Clowns

Me: Hey God.

God: Hey John.

Me: I'm tired of seeing clowns all over the news. They are all totally freaking me out.

God: I get that.

Me: Those fake painted on-smiles are totally creepy. I can't tell who is really beneath them.

God: I agree. Super disturbing.

Me: When are all these clowns finally going to go away?

God: Right after election day.

Me: Phew!

Sledgehammers

Me: Hey God.

God: Hey John.

Me: Anxiety has me trapped inside my own head. It's like I'm in a maze. I just keep running around, but I never find a way out. So many walls. I'm surrounded by dead ends. I'm lost and exhausted.

God: I'm coming. Hang tight.

Me: Great! Are you going to show me the way out?

God: No. There is no way out of this maze...

Me: Dang.

God: Yet.

Me: Yet?

God: Yeah. I'm bringing a sledgehammer.

Fitting In

Me: Hey God.

God: Hey John.

Me: I don't fit in.

God: You're welcome!

Rise

Me: Hey Regret.

Regret: Hey John.

Me: You are the reason I can't move on with my life.

Regret: Really? What did I do?

Me: You won't let go of me. I'm stuck.

Regret: There is only one problem with that.

Me: What's that?

Regret: I don't have any arms. I can't keep you here.

Me: Then why aren't I moving?

Regret: Because you are the one holding on to me. I'm ready to go, but you won't release me from your tight grip. There is nothing I want more than to disappear. Let me go. Let me vanish.

Me: I'm afraid.

Regret: Why?

Me: Because I don't think I know how to walk away from you.

Regret: Oh, you aren't going to be walking.

Me: I'm not?

Regret: Nope. You're gonna rise!

Me: How?

God: I'll show you.

Me: Oh...hey God.

God: Release regret from your fist. Come with Me. We can rise.

Me: Is it that simple?

God: Yes. Take My hand. Hold on to it as tightly as you did to regret and I'll show you all that you've been missing.

Me: Where are we going?

God: Everywhere.

Me: I'm ready.

Regret: See ya never.

Me: See ya never.

God: Rise. Rise. Rise.

Cruelty

Me: Hey God.

God: Hey John.

Me: Sometimes people say the cruelest things to each other.

God: I know. It's often an indication of a battle raging inside them.

Me: How should I respond to someone who is angry and bitter?

God: With words of great kindness and generosity.

Me: Will that change them?

God: Probably not, but it will change you.

Where Is My Mind?

Me: Hey God.

God: Hey John.

Me: I'm not sure I can keep talking with You like this any longer.

God: Why is that?

Me: I think these conversations with You are making me lose my mind.

God: Nah.

Me: But something is happening in me.

God: That's true. Something is changing within you, but you're not losing your mind. Don't fret.

Me: If I am not losing my mind, what's happening to me?

God: You're just finding your heart.

Get Up!

Me: Hey God.

God: Hey John.

Me: I don't want to get out of bed today.

God: Sorry, no time to waste, you have to get moving! I have a job for you today.

Me: What is it?

God: I need you to put your feet on the floor and go outside to embrace this sacred day I have created for you. I need you to look for Me in the wonder of creation. I need you to hear My voice in the cries of the suffering. I need you to take a few moments and be still so you can feel My quiet presence in your heart. I need you to quit standing on the riverbank of life watching life pass you by. It's time to step into the current and to allow the water of life carry you from river bend to river bend. There is nothing left for you on the shore. Enter the flow. See what is waiting for you. Come to Me. Embrace this wondrous day. I need you to serve others. I need you to discover your purpose. Jump in! Let's go! I love you! I need you to join the adventure! Let's go!

Me: Huh. That seems like a lot.

God: It really isn't.

Me: One quick question. Will doing any of that require me to put on my pants?

God: Preferably.

Storms

Me: Hey God.

God: Hey John.

Me: This storm came out of nowhere!

God: Don't worry.

Me: Why?

God: All storms pass.

Me: But this one is particularly scary.

God: All storms pass.

Me: Uh huh...but I'm having a hard time seeing the road ahead.

God: All storms pass.

Me: You're not just talking about the weather, are You?

God: You're finally starting to get the hang of these conversations.

Me: It only took two years...

God: All storms pass?

Me: All storms pass!

Unspoken Words

Me: Hey God.

God: Hey John.

Me: My mom died five years ago today and I'm still grieving.

God: That's a good sign.

Me: Of what?

God: That she was a good mother.

Me: I was not the best son.

God: You showed her that she was loved. That is the greatest gift you can give anybody.

Me: I just wish grief didn't hurt so much.

God: There is no greater pain than to have willfully given a piece of your heart to somebody, only to watch them pass away.

Me: I left so many words unspoken between us.

God: That is the trick with relationships, isn't it? You always assume there is enough time to say everything you need to those you love, when you have no idea how much time is left together in your shared stories. You think that your time together is infinite, but it's not. Oftentimes you leave tender words unsaid, embraces not given and pardons not offered because you think you can do it the next day. The problem is, there isn't always a tomorrow. Don't procrastinate with your beloveds. Tell the meaningful people in your life that you love them. Do it today. Don't leave anything unsaid or undone. If you love somebody, tell them immediately. Don't wait. Forgive somebody today. Don't wait. Mercy and love should be offered at every chance. Take stock of the people you love and tell them.

Me: I understand.

God: Remember, death isn't the end.

Me: Right. Can you tell my mom I miss her?

God: I think she would love for you to say that yourself.

Me: Hey Mom.

Mom: Hey John.

Me: I love you.

Mom: I love you, too. You really should shave. You look like a serial killer.

Me: Ah. I've missed you.

Mom: I know.

You Have The Right To Remain Silent

Me: Hey God.

God:

Me: Hey God?

God:

Me: Hey God?!

God:

Me: Hey God??!!!

God:

Me: Where are You?????!!

God: I'm here.

Me: Where have You been?! I've been trying to talk to You for days!

God: I know.

Me: You know?!

God: Yep. You've had quite a bit to say.

Me: That's outrageous! I've gone through two notebooks! And You've just sat there and let me yammer on without saying anything back to me?!

God: Pretty much.

Me: Why??!!!

God: Because you never leave any space in our conversations for Me to respond to you.

Me: Oh.

God: Try being quiet for a while and listening for My voice.

Me: I'll try...but silence makes me uncomfortable.

God: It's not the silence that makes you uncomfortable. You feel that way because of what I'm trying to tell you.

Me: What are you trying to tell me?

God: A bunch of things.

Me: Like?

God: I want to tell you that you are a gift to this world. That you are good. That you are loved. That I am proud of you. That I forgive you. That I made you to be more than you have settled for. That I need you to love other people and give your compassion and care more freely. Everybody deserves your empathy. I want to tell you that it's time to rise and build the life you deserve. I want to tell you that life on Earth is too short to waste on fear and regret. I want you to know that you will face more suffering in the future, but you need not fret, because I will always be right next to you. I want you to know that you are worthy of love and that despair's only power over you is what you have freely given to it.

Me: Ugh. You're right. All of that does make me feel uncomfortable.

God: I know. That is why you keep talking over My voice. You aren't afraid of the silence, you're afraid of what I need to tell you.

Me: What should I do?

God: Find a quiet place and close your mouth for a little bit so we can work on opening your heart.

Me:

God: Sound good?

Me:

God: Nice. This is going to take a while. First, you are loved. You are loved beyond measure. I am here. I have so many things to tell you.

Work Of The Soul

Me: Hey God.

God: Hey John.

Me: Our world is so ugly.

God: Ugly? No, it is just the opposite.

Me: Uh, when was the last time You watched the news?

God: I've never watched the news.

Me: That means You don't really know what's going on right now!

God: I know exactly what's going on.

Me: Prove it!

God: Right now, there is a homeless woman being cared for by a volunteer named Allison in a shelter. They are sharing a couple of bowls of turkey soup together under a flickering fluorescent light. In a few minutes, they're going to be surprised when they discover that they are both widows. For the next hour they're going to talk and tell stories about their deceased beloveds. They are going to laugh and cry. Right now, in that shelter, these two lovely women are connecting with, and serving one another other profoundly. That's what's happening in the world. It's not ugly. It's beautiful.

Me: Yes, but didn't you see that report on terrorism last night that said –

God: I didn't see that. But I did see a baby giggling for the first time this morning in an apartment in India. His face exploded with joy and gladness because of the silly sounds his older sister was making. I love watching little babies laugh, especially when they've never done it before. It was pure and simple. In just a couple of moments the entire family gathered around him and all took turns making crazy noises to keep him laughing. It was beautiful. When was the last time you made a baby laugh? When was the last time you exposed yourself to that kind of radiant happiness?

Me: I can't remember – although, that's not the point. How can you not see what's going on out there?

God: You know what I can see right now? I see life. I see miracles. I see a bright red hummingbird flirting with a pastel yellow sunflower. I see an excited teenage girl filling out her application to go to college so she can follow her dream of becoming a doctor. I see an elderly couple holding hands on a park bench. I can see a two-hundred-year-old tree being climbed by a couple of children. I can see the vast ocean meeting the shoreline and 1 hear the tide splash against the rocks. I can see the moon and the sun and the endless network of galaxies around your blue, spinning planet. I can see all of the atoms that make up who you are. All of it is a miracle. Miracles are all I see. I see life. I see courage. I see people connecting and helping each other. I see creation. I see love. I don't see ugly. I see beauty. Remarkable beauty.

Me: What about all the horrible things? Are You just ignoring them?

God: No. I see those too and I am just as fully present in those dark moments, but you have started to believe that is all there is.

Me: I know...

God: There is more light and goodness in your world than there are shadows and violence. Quit fixing your gaze on the darkness. There is nothing that will feed you there. Put your eyes upon the miracles that surround you. If you baptize yourself in the toxic fear and pessimism of the news, you will unknowingly become an evangelist for it.

Me: I have been kind of a prophet of doom lately...

God: The world is so incredibly beautiful and I have placed constant reminders of that fact all around you. I want you to spend the rest of your day listening for and looking for beauty. Turn off the "scary news" and start being a witness to all the good news that is happening right now before your own eyes. I want you to report back later with what you find.

Me: This sounds like homework.

God: I call it soulwork.

Breaking Up

Me: Hey God.

God: Hey John.

Me: I'm breaking up with You.

God: Again?

Me: Yep.

God: This is the fourth time today.

Me: I know.

God: And it's not even 7am yet.

Me: I know.

God: Does that mean that you want Me to quit carrying you?

Me: I didn't say that! I still need You to carry me up this hill. I can't do it on my own – it's steep!

God: Okay. Hang on.

Me: I guess I'll give You another chance.

God: What?

Me: I want to get back together.

God: Great! Stay close! This part of the climb is tricky. Lots of slippery rock and an irritable bear waiting to attack you up behind those trees over there.

Me: Okay, but can't you go any faster? This is taking a lot longer than I thought it would.

God: Relax. Enjoy the view. We'll get to the top soon. Just be patient.

Me: I'm not good at being patient. I feel really frustrated.

God: Uh oh, does that mean -

Me: Yep. I'm breaking up with You!

God: Again?

Me: Yep.

God: Okay. Shall I stop carrying you now?

Me: Uh – can You bring me a bit further?

God: It'd be my pleasure. Hang on.

Hey God. Hey John.
🌐 Public

Me: The world is a mess.

God: Yeah - things do seem to be a little unhinged right now.

Me: Can't You intervene and help us out?

God: I already did.

Me: What did You do?

God: I made you.

Add to your post   🖼 📹 📍 😀

Q W E R T Y U I O P

Love Machine

Me: Hey God.

God: Hey John.

Me: Why am I so sad today?

God: Because you refuse to love everyone.

Me: No, I don't. I'm a love machine!

God: Er...

Me: You know what I mean. I am really doing my best to show love to everyone I meet. I know that I'm not perfect, but I'm working on it.

God: Everyone? I disagree. You withhold your love. You pick and choose the people you think deserve your empathy and compassion. You act as if love should be reserved for those who have done something to deserve it. You treat love like a finite commodity that you need to ration. It's not. Love is the ultimate renewable resource. You are called to love everyone.

Me: And like I just said – I'm trying to love everyone!

God: Everyone?

Me: Yeppers.

God: Even yourself?

Me: What? That doesn't count.

God: It counts double. You won't know how to share love with anybody else if you can't share it with yourself first. How can you and I have a relationship, if you don't love the person that I made you to be? You are sad because you have denied yourself access to the same care and dignity that you attempt to show other people. You are sad because you are trying to serve others with hands you don't respect, which makes you a bit of a hypocrite.

Me: Wait – is this a Tough Love Monday thing?

God: You know it. Buckle up.

Me: Great...

God: You can't talk about loving anybody else until you love yourself. You can't love Me fully until you learn to love your own self. I made you. And you are called to love what I have made. I was the potter and you were my clay. Do you really hate the art that I have created?

Me: No... I'll try to be kinder to myself.

God: The time for trying is over. Do you want to know what it is like to live a joyful life? Do you want to know what it is like to be able to get out of bed in the morning with a heart of abundant exuberance?

Me: Of course.

God: All of that begins with self-love. Love every part of yourself. Even your weaknesses and failings. Love your ugly as much as your beauty. Love it all. Care for yourself. Show yourself mercy. Forgive yourself. Be charitable to your soul. The sadness you feel inside will melt away once you offer yourself just an ounce of love. You are so thirsty for self-respect. Let yourself drink from the well of love. Drink it in and discover joy. Let joy surprise you with what I have in store for you. Let joy lead you to the life of service that you claim you want. The best thing about living a life of joy is that you will never surrender to fear again. Joy keeps coming and coming like the tide. Love thyself and know true joy.

Me: I will.

God: Then you can finally live your calling.

Me: What calling is that?

God: As a love machine.

Me: Sweet. I'll make t-shirts!

Falling Skies

Me: Hey God.

God: Hey John.

Me: The sky is falling!

God: Nah.

Me: Yes, it is!

God: Relax, Chicken Licken. The sky is right where it's supposed to be.

Me: What's happening then?

God: The sky isn't falling. You're just rising up into it.

Me: I'm getting vertigo, don't let me fall!

God: Chill. I would never let you fall. I'm the one who is lifting you up.

Me: How high are we going to fly?

God: I was about to ask you that same question.

Survive To Share

Me: Hey God.

God: Hey John.

Me: Why do You allow me to have depression?

God: So that you could find a way to survive it.

Me: There have been times recently when I felt like my whole body was being poisoned. It's like there was a knife in my stomach and my brain was on fire. All I could do was lie on the floor, wracked with pain.

God: You survived that.

Me: Sometimes I feel nothing at all. Just abject emptiness. A deep loneliness where I float alone inside an empty oblivion. Like there was nothing inside me, as I was without a soul. I'm covered in darkness and devoid of emotion. Feeling nothing is even worse than any pain I've ever endured.

God: You survived that as well.

Me: But even though I'm doing okay right now, I know that depression will be back to wrap its icy fingers around my throat once more. It's hard to relax because it's only a matter of time until it shows up again.

God: And when it does, you will survive it again.

Me: I just want to know why You allow me to go through all of this!

God: I already answered that. You are suffering through depression so that you can survive it.

Me: And then what?

God: Then you can tell people who are going through the exact same thing how you survived.

Me: Oh.

God: There is no better storyteller than those who have survived something extraordinarily painful.

Me: Fine. What do I do now?

God: Keep surviving and share your story. Survive and be a storyteller. Survive and share. Survive and share.

Problems

Me: Hey God.

God: Hey John.

Me: I've got problems!

God: Sounds dramatic.

Me: Oh, it is!

God: I bet I can get everything going on with you today boiled down to just one main problem.

Me: No way! I have hundreds of them! I'm complicated! I have serious issues to deal with!

God: What's up?

Me: My life is out of control!

God: That sounds like the makings of an incredible adventure!

Me: Uh, my life ain't an adventure!

God: Yes, it is. All life is an adventure. It's about hunting for treasure, exploring the world, serving and protecting people, fighting dragons, getting lost in the wild for a bit, discovering your purpose, and growing into a hero while trusting that miracles will arrive when you feel like all hope is lost. That is all adventure!

Me: I don't want adventure today – I just want to get by!

God: And there is your main problem!

Frozen

Me: Hey God.

God: Hey John.

Me: Ugh.

God: What's up?

Me: I'm frozen.

God: I'm working on it. The light is coming.

Me: I'm talking about my heart.

God: So am I.

Healing

Me: Hey God.

God: Hey John.

God: Why are you sitting there all alone in the pitch dark?

Me: I'm hiding so that nothing can hurt me.

God: The dark won't prevent you from being hurt. You can still be wounded in there, you just won't see it coming. Come out. The light is waiting.

Me: No. I told you, I don't want to. I'm afraid of being hurt out there in the light.

God: Stop fibbing. You aren't afraid of being hurt out here.

Me: What am I afraid of then?

God: Being healed.

Me: Oh...right...

God: Wounds will never heal until you let them. Scars will never form until you look at them in the light. You'll never be able to forgive yourself cloistered in the dark. Forgiveness and healing are fruits of the light. Come out. Come out. It's time. I love you. Come out!

Me: I don't think I can. I've gotten too used to it in here.

God: Yes, you can. I'll give you new eyes so that you can finally see yourself the way that I do:

Beautiful.
Worthy.
Brave.
Forgiven.
Come out. Come out.
I love you.
Come out!

Holding For Sunrise

Me: Hey God.

God: Hey John.

Me: I am having a hard time talking with You lately.

God: I've noticed.

Me: In fact, just typing this out makes me feel sick to my stomach.

God: It's okay. I understand.

Me: Do You understand?! I'm really suffering!

God: I love you. Don't give up. You don't have to say anything to Me. Just hold on.

Me: I don't think I've ever felt so broken. This is the coldest, pitch-darkest of nights that I've ever experienced.

God: I know, but the darkness is nearly done teaching you what you needed to learn. The pain you've been enduring is almost over. It's time to let the light have its turn with you. You have learned what it is like to live in the desert. It's time to come and drink from the spring.

Me: Why did you abandon me in my darkest of nights!?

God: I didn't. I've been right here next to you painting the most beautiful of sunrises that you'll ever see.

Me: I can't wait...

God: Hold on. I love you. Don't surrender to the shadows. Remember that the light always pushes out the dark. Grey is giving way to pink and orange and yellow daybreak. Hold on.

The Present

Me: Hey God.

God: Hey John.

Me: I can't focus today.

God: That's because you never spend any time in "today".

Me: That makes zero sense. If I'm not in today, where am I?

God: You're more of a tomorrow and yesterday kind of guy. Which seems appropriate since you are such a prolific time traveler.

Me: I am? That sounds cool! Do I get to wear some awesome time-traveling goggles?

God: It's not cool. You spend all your days visiting your past so you can fret over the mistakes that you've made and then you spend all of your nights traveling to the future, so you can worry about what hasn't happened yet. You are never in the present. You are never aware of the graces that I'm constantly showering you with because you are too busy torturing yourself in the distant past or in the unknown future.

Me: I can't help it...

God: Knock it off. Of course you can help it. You keep choosing to live in yesterday's regret and you concern yourself with things that may or may not happen tomorrow. You are living in every time except for the here and now. You are stuck in a time loop that you can't ever break until you follow my instructions.

Me: Which instructions are those?

God: Go find a mirror. Look into it and with absolute sincerity, say the following:

I choose to live in this moment.
I choose to fall in love with the present.
There is mercy in this moment.
I can't change or control
what I've done in my past.
I've made so many terrible mistakes.
I'm sorry.
I will do better.
I forgive myself.
I've hurt so many people.
I'm sorry.
I will do better.
I forgive myself.
In my past other people have

hurt me both intentionally and unintentionally.
I'm letting go of my anger towards them.
I'm releasing my resentments.
It's all a poison and I'm done with it.
I'm leaving my yesterday in the past.
I choose to live in this moment.
I can't change or control
what may happen to me tomorrow.
The only thing I can control is how
prepared I am to meet the challenges
that are ahead of me.
I refuse to waste my life
worrying about what hasn't happened yet.
No matter what comes my way
I know that I won't be alone.
I am loved.
I am loved.
Nothing can touch me for
I am loved beyond measure.
I am loved.
In this present moment
I am surrounded by miracles
And hope
And beauty
And promise
And opportunity
And mercy

And forgiveness.
The more time
I spend in the past
Or in the future
The less I'm aware of the graces of life
that surround me right now.
Right now
I'm loved.
Right now
I'm okay.
Right now
God is here.
Right now
I'm safe.
Right now
I am loved.
I am loved beyond measure.

Me: I don't think I can get through all of that without crying.

God: Say it all. It's the only way you'll accept the gift I have for you.

Me: You got me a gift?

God: Yep. It's called the present for a reason.

ME: Hey God.

God: Hey John.

ME: I'm sad. I'm afraid.
I'm broken. I'm paralyzed.
I'm ruined. I'm depressed.

God: I'm Here!!!

Someday Can't Wait

Me: Hey God.

God: Hey John.

Me: Thanks for being so patient with me while I try to figure out my life.

God: You bet!

Me: Someday I'll start living the life that You created me for. Someday I'll celebrate the miracles in my life instead of focusing on what I think I lack. Someday I'll love other people unconditionally. Someday I will view my life as a joyful adventure and not just something to survive. Someday I'll take the risk to follow my dreams. Someday I won't ignore the love song that You sing to me.

God: Awesome! That sounds great. I literally have ALL THE TIME to wait for those things to finally happen. There's just one little problem...

Me: What's that?

God: You don't have all the time to wait. I am infinite. You aren't.

Me: Ack!

God: There's no day but today. You keep putting everything that you'd like for yourself off until some magical day in the future. You only get so many "somedays" and eventually you'll run out of them. I can wait until someday for you to remember who you were born to be, but you can't! Your clock is ticking. Why not replace someday with TODAY?

Me: Because that would be scary.

God: Don't be scared to do everything in your power to lead an authentic and happy life. Be scared not to.

Me: Right.

God: Now, go back and change all your somedays with today.

Me: TODAY I'll start living the life that You created me for. TODAY I'll celebrate the miracles in my life instead of focusing on what I think I lack. TODAY I'll love other people unconditionally. TODAY I will view my life as a joyful adventure and not just something to survive. TODAY I'll risk following my dreams. TODAY I won't ignore the love song that You sing to me.

HEY GOD. HEY JOHN.

God: There is no day but -
Me: TODAY!
God: Today! Today! Today!

Honey, have you seen my God?

Me: Hey God.

God: Hey John.

Me: I can't find You anywhere!

God: Keep looking!

Me: Where are You in my life?

God: That depends.

Me: On what?

God: On where you last put Me.

The River

Me: Hey God.

God: Hey John.

Me: I can't sleep. I'm too angry with You.

God: I know you are.

Me: We talk and we talk and it seems like nothing ever really changes in my life.

God: I know it does.

Me: I feel like I'm floating in this vast river and no matter how hard I swim, I keep drifting away from You.

God: You can't drift away from Me.

Me: Why not?

God: Because I Am The River.

Me: Then why am I struggling so much?

God: Because you're swimming in the wrong direction. Stop thrashing. Stop kicking. Fall into My current and let Me carry you to where I need you to go.

Me: And where exactly are You are taking me?

God: To Glory.

Proof That You Have Loved

Me: Hey God.

God: Hey John.

Me: I just have one simple request today.

God: Alrighty, let's hear it.

Me: Can you make sure that I never get hurt again?

God: Nope.

Me: Uh, fine. Can you at least take away the emotion of grief from me?

God: Nope. Sorrow and grief are proof that you have risked your heart to love somebody else. The more scars you end up with on your heart, the better. It proves that you remained vulnerable to the world. A closed heart may never get hurt, but it also will never feel the joy of connecting deeply with another person. A closed heart never serves. Grief is the cost of unconditional love. Grief is a gift. Grief is a reminder that life is precious.

Me: You want me to grieve?

God: I want you to love unconditionally and grief is proof that you did.

Me: Well, I've been offering a lot of proof of that lately...

God: Keep up the good work!

Slam Poetry

Me: Hey God.

Depression: Hey John.

Me: I thought you were giving me the day off?

Depression: I am, but before I go, I wanted to read you a quick poem that I wrote just for you.

Me: Fine, if that's what it will take for you to leave me alone. Let's hear it.

Depression: I'm so nervous! Okay – here it goes:

"Someday you'll be invisible"
by Depression

Today is going to be terrible
And it's all your fault.
You suck.
Your life sucks.
And nothing you will ever
Do will matter.
– Nothing.

I will shrink you until
You disappear forever.
Nobody will care when you're gone.

– Nobody.

You're worthless.
You're alone.
You're without talent.
You will never be happy.
The emptiness inside you is permanent.
Don't leave your couch.
Don't leave your house.
Stay right there.
You are mine.
I own you.
Someday I'll erase you.
I can't wait
For you to be gone.
– For you to become invisible.

Me: Ugh. That is not a nice poem.

Depression: Thanks!

Me: You can leave now.

Depression: I won't be far away. Enjoy the day off! Expect me all the earlier tomorrow! Don't leave your couch! I mean it!

God: Hey John.

Me: I just got done talking with Depression.

HEY GOD. HEY JOHN.

God: I heard everything. Don't fret because Depression is a liar. I wrote a poem too.

Me: You and I have been having a poetry theme lately.

God: I know! I love poetry!

Me: Alright, I guess I should hear the poem you wrote for me.

God: You don't understand, YOU are My poem. You are a carefully crafted piece of art. The poetry of who you are is unique. I have written no other poem like yours. Every word of love and hope that I have delicately inscribed on the walls of your heart is true. No matter how dark the world gets, your poem will be read because I've written your life with My light.

Me: I'm a glow-in-the-dark poem?

God: Yes and the name of your poem is "I have survived the dark night because I am loved beyond measure."

Me: That's sort of a long title.

God: It needs a long title because you are going to have a long life. You have to remember that. I need you to keep working on finding joy. I need you to be My hands on Earth. Don't give up.

Don't give into despair. Fire up your heart with light so that the darkness can't swallow you up without getting massive indigestion. You are my poem. Your life is a sonnet. I used My love for you to write you into existence.

Me: What do I do now?

God: Get off the couch and go stand outside in the sunlight for ten minutes.

Me: Why?

God: Because My poetry shines brightest in the sunlight.

How My Prayer Life
Usually Works

Me:

God: Hey John.

Me: Not today. I'm not in the mood.

God: Hey John.

Me: Seriously...just let me be.

God: Hey John.

Me: I don't want to talk!

God: Hey John.

Me:

God: Hey John. Hey John. Hey John. Hey John. Hey John. Hey John. Hey John. Hey John. Hey John. Hey John. Hey John. Hey John. Hey -

Me: LEAVE ME ALONE!!! I DON'T WANT TO TALK WITH YOU!!! I JUST WANT TO BE LEFT ALONE!!! I CAN HANDLE THIS ON MY OWN!!!

God: Gotcha.

Me:

God: Hey John.

Me: Whew...

More Than Air

Me: Hey God.

God: Hey John.

Me: My anxiety is crushing me today. I'm not sure I can survive this.

God: Breathe. In and out. Slowly. You are going to be fine. Breathe in. And exhale it all out. Breathe.

Me: I can't!!

God: Take a couple of deep breaths. Breathe in and breathe out. Your heart will calm down if you just breathe deeply and allow yourself to be healed.

Me: I don't think air is going to heal me this time.

God: I didn't say anything about air.

Me: What am I breathing in, then?

God: Me.

My Hypocrisy

Me: Hey God.

God: Hey John.

Me: I think that I'm finally finished with these conversations with You.

God: You can't quit. We're not done.

Me: We aren't?

God: Nope. Not even close.

Me: I can't do it any longer. After almost two years of doing this I'm tired of feeling like such a hypocrite.

God: How are you a hypocrite?

Me: Because even though I've posted over 600 of our conversations, I am still plagued by such overwhelming doubt in You. I keep pouring out my heart to You in the hope that I can overcome my despair, but that hasn't happened. I worry that these conversations are just a sign that I'm losing my mind.

God: You're not losing your mind, you're just losing some parts of your ego. You are having a hard time coming to grips with the idea that you aren't in control of everything. You are also finding it hard to believe that you are worthy of being loved unconditionally.

Me: I am always wondering if You are listening to me. I have wept tears that I wonder if you've ever seen.

God: Of course I have. I've heard everything. I'm right here. I love you. I'm listening. You aren't ever alone. I love you.

Me: I wish I could completely believe all of that. It would offer such a comfort to me.

God: Someday you will believe in all of that. Just keep showing up. Keep an open mind about Me.

Me: But what about all of my doubts?

God: Keep those too. Keep talking to Me. Keep asking questions. Remain curious. I am not afraid of your doubts. I love them. They show that you are hard at work. I'd be more concerned if you didn't have any uncertainties. Doubt is the uneven path to true faith. Stay on the path. One foot in front of the other. One day at a time. One doubt after another. Keep working. I love you. Keep working.

Me: I don't know if I can.

God: I do. Coming to understand Me and My love for you will be the adventure of your life. Don't quit on Me. I have so much that I still want to show you.

Me: I feel like such a hypocrite though.

God: You're not a hypocrite. You're just a work in progress. You are a piece of unfinished art that I'm not done with yet.

Me: You're not?

God: Nope. Not even close.

ME: Hey God

God: Hey John.

ME: ~~Help me fit in~~

ME: ~~Help me be normal.~~

ME: ~~Help me act just like everybody else.~~

ME: ~~Help me do what people expect of me.~~

ME: Help me shine!

God: I thought you'd never ask!!

Wall Of Shouting

Me: Hey God.

God: Hey John.

Me: Everybody is so angry at each other today.

God: I know.

Me: There is a huge wall of noise that has been built from people just shouting over each other.

God: All will be well. People will come together eventually.

Me: They will?! I can't imagine how that could be possible. We are all just screaming at one another. Nothing ever changes.

God: Things will change. The way you are all treating each other is unsustainable. Eventually mankind will give up always trying to "win" an argument and will start to enjoy the fruit that comes from really listening to the people who disagree with you. Eventually you'll be tired of being misused by people in power who count on you all not listening to each other. Eventually you will really start to hear one another and your shared aims of love and service.

Me: Maybe You could speed up the process and help us learn to listen to each other a little more quickly?

God: I've already given you all the tools you need to learn how to listen. I gave you a 2:1 ears to mouth ratio. You were created to listen more and talk less. Plus, I also gave you something else when your mouth gets too far ahead of your ears.

Me: What's that?

God: Duct tape.

Both Things At Once

Me: Hey God.

God: Hey John.

Me: I am completely broken.

God: Yep, but I still think that you're beautiful.

Me: Um? What? Look at me. I feel like a piece of shattered glass. I am an absolute mess.

God: Sure, but you are still beautiful to Me.

Me: Please quit saying that. I just want You to repair me.

God: Nope.

Me: Why not?

God: Because I still think that –

Me: Don't say it!

God – you're beautiful.

Me: *sigh* Just put the pieces of my life back together the way they were before I was broken.

God: No can do.

Me: Please?! I feel like I've been smashed into a million small pieces.

God: You were.

Me: So fix me then!

God: Nothing to fix. You are still beautiful.

Me: What about all of my wounds? What about all of my scars and fractures? What about all the times I've had my heart broken? Those things aren't beautiful.

God: Those are exactly what make you beautiful. Yes, you have been shattered and crushed into tiny bits BUT you have survived. The fissures in your heart are proof of the courage you've shown in the face of despair. The places in your life where you have been broken have been rearranged into a piece of art that tells your story of perseverance and hope. You have survived the darkest of nights and there is nothing more beautiful than that.

Me: I just don't know who I am anymore.

God: Yes, you do. You are a work of art. You are broken and you are beautiful. You can be both of those things at the same time.

Me: Okay...

God: Say it.

Me: I am broken. I am beautiful. I can be both of those things at the same time.

God: Again.

Me: I am broken. I am beautiful. I can be both of those things at the same time.

God: Nice job.

Me: Now what?

God: Now, you need to get somebody else to say to say that exact same thing.

Me: Hey reader. Repeat after me:

You are broken. You are beautiful. You can be both of those things at the same time.

You:

More Than I Can Handle

Me: Hey God.

God: Hey John.

Me: I thought we had a deal?!

God: What are you talking about?

Me: You said that You weren't ever going to give me more than I could handle.

God: I haven't.

Me: Then You and I have a pretty different idea of how much I can handle.

God: Clearly.

Me: I cannot possibly deal with the problem that came my way today.

God: Yes you can, but only if you finally start to see yourself in the way that I do. You have a deep well of strength inside you that you've never tapped into. I made you with the courage of a hundred lions.

Me: If that is true, why don't I ever feel brave?

God: Because you choose to believe all of the lies told to you by your self-doubt and fear. You have decided to accept the cruel falsehood that you are broken and less than other people. You refuse to acknowledge your brilliant, luminescent soul that cannot be dimmed by the shadows of this world. You believe in the whispered lie that you don't have the power to stand up again when you are knocked down. You believe there are problems that are too big for you and I to handle together.

Me: I'm hopeless...

God: No, you are just the opposite! You are stitched together with nothing but hope! You just don't realize how magnificent and courageous you are. Remind yourself daily that there is nothing in your life that you can't handle. Remember the strength that I gave you at birth.

Me: I have a terrible memory for remembering anything good about myself when trouble comes.

God: I have an idea. Grab that pen. I have something that I want you to write down so you can remember it whenever you face something that scares you. Write down part of the code that I wrote inside the wall of your heart when I created you.

Me: Okay – let me grab some paper...

God: Paper won't work this time.

Me: What are we writing this on??
God: Trust me..

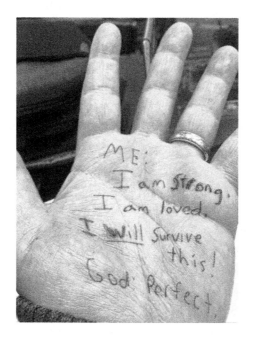

Still Alive

Me: Hey God.

God: Hey John.

Me: Why can't I stop crying?

God: Because you are trying to. You can't keep hiding from your pain. Give it oxygen.

Me: I am such a mess.

God: A perfectly imperfect, beautiful, chaotic mess.

Me: I don't want to feel like this anymore.

God: Then it's time for you to allow yourself to really cry. Sob away and listen to the messages that the tears on your cheek have been trying to tell you for the past few years.

Me: Which messages are those?

God: That you are so much stronger than you can ever imagine. Each tear that falls is evidence of your courage in the face of suffering and proof that you're still fighting. Each tear screams to the world that you are still alive! Tears are your medal of valor. Tears are the testimony you give on how you have endured the wars in your heart and in the world. Tears are proof that you haven't surrendered your humanity and you still care...and love...and you are still connected to your soul. Tears prove that you are still vulnerable and that you haven't erected a wall around yourself. Those are just a few of the messages that have been scrawled inside the tears in your face.

Me: I just hope I survive my depression.

God: You have. I can tell because you're crying!

Me: Tears are proof of survival?

God: Yes!!!

Me: I hope I'm always strong enough to cry when I need to.

God: You will be. Spend a moment and listen to the message of your tears:

> *Keep crying. You will rise again.*
> *You are stronger than you know.*
> *You have survived the dark night.*
> *You are still alive. You are still alive.*
> *Keep crying. You will rise again.*
> *You are loved.*

Me: Amen...

Disturbed

Me: Hey God.

God: Hey John.

Me: Before you say anything, I just realized that my shirt is on backwards.

God: And it's inside out as well.

Me: Really?! I've been out all morning! Has anybody noticed?

God: Just the people who have eyes.

Me: Great...I have been having a hard time focusing lately. My thoughts have been a bit jumbled.

God: That's because you are disturbed.

Me: I'm disturbed?

God: Yes.

Me: That's not very nice!

God: I mean that as a compliment. I'm not talking about your state of mind or mental health being disturbed – although...

Me: I know...I'm working on being kind to myself.

God: What I mean is the reason you can't focus right now is because your soul is disturbed. It's unsettled.

Me: So, what You are saying is that I'm spiritually disturbed?

God: Exactly!

Me: Ugh...that sounds terrible. Can you cure it?

God: No cure is needed. Your soul is being woken up from a long slumber. The waters of your soul are covered in ripples because something is moving within you.

Me: I don't want to be disturbed!

God: Yes, you do. It just means that your soul is stirring. You are almost ready.

Me: For what?!

God: To become a serious disturbance for other people in need.

Me: I don't understand...

God: The world needs people to listen to what their souls are working so hard to tell them. Your souls are becoming restless and they are ready to get to work. Hurry! The world needs you! It's time to act. It's time to serve and to love each other without fear. The time has come to break through complacency and start making some ripples and then waves that will awaken each other. Become a disruption of service, forgiveness and compassion. Your soul is disturbed and it's ready to get to work. The world can't wait anymore. It needs you. I need you. I have no hands but yours. Be My song.

Me: What can I do? I'm just one small, broken person?

God: There are two important things you can do to help the world.

Me: What are they?

God: First, flip your way of thinking. You can do more than you have ever imagined. Recognize that the life I gave you is a gift and it's up to you to pass on that gift. Every life is a gift. There are people reading this right now that you will never meet and their life is a gift too! They feel the same disturbance within them. They are also hearing their call to act, to forgive, to serve, to love, and to turn the miracle of their lives into a gift for other people. You are all called to change this world through the gift of your life! You are called to make a joyful disturbance!

Me: Sounds like an adventure!

God: You have no idea!

Me: Alright...You said that there were two things that I need to do to help the world. What's the second thing I can do?

God: Fix your shirt. It looks like you were dressed by a badger.

Me: Right.

What Defines Me?

Me: Hey God.

God: Hey John.

Me: I didn't become the person I wanted to be.

God: Who do you think you've become?

Me: A man paralyzed by fear and anxiety.

God: That's not who you are, they are just what you are experiencing right now. You are more than that. You won't be defined by the riptide trying to pull you out to sea.

Me: What will I be defined by?

God: By how hard you swim to get back to the shore. Quit making your current experience your identity. Remember who I made you to be.

Me: I'm not sure who that is.

God: You are a survivor and a warrior. That's who you are. You aren't your diagnosis or your mistakes or the bad things that have happened to you. Those aren't who you are. You are so much more!! You are My treasured masterpiece, created out of nothing but love and light. Listen to Me right now, you are strong. You are someone who will keep kicking and fighting until you break free from the riptide and return to dry land.

You will endure and find peace on the other side of suffering. Stay the course. You are on the verge of becoming the person you have longed to be. The day is coming when I introduce you to somebody that you absolutely must meet! They are one of my favorite people! You're gonna love them once you come to know them!

Me: Who is this awesome person?

God: You.

Candlelight

Me: Hey God.

God: Hey John.

Me: I am going to give up.

God: You can't. Don't surrender to the darkness.

Me: I'm sorry. I just can't hold on any longer.

God: Then let Me hold on to you. I need you. I will lift you up like a lit candle.

Me: What good will that do?

God: You can become a guiding light for somebody else who feels the same despair as you do. You can be an example of how a single light can survive a dark night. You can show others that if you can hold on, so can they.

Me: I'm too weak to be of any use.

God: Even the faintest of light can be all another person needs to be reminded of how a glimmer of hope can outlast any gathering shadow. You need to survive so you can become a beacon for somebody else.

Me: Then what?

God: Then that person will become a light for another person and so on until the entire world is lit up by billions of soft little candles. Listen to Me when I tell you this:

There is nothing more contagious than hope.

Simply Must Do

Me: Hey God.

God: Hey John.

Me: I'm not leaving my room today.

God: You have to. There is too much waiting for you out there.

Me: I'm too scared.

God:

Sometimes the thing that scares you the most is the thing you simply *must do!*

Fit Out

Me: Hey God.

God: Hey John.

Me: I am afraid that I'll ~~never~~ fit in

God: Let me edit that for you.

> *There is nothing*
> *more boring*
> *than trying to*
> *become something*
> *other than the*
> *unique creation*
> *you were made to be.*
>
> *So follow your heart.*

ME: Hey God.
God: Hey John.
Stress: Hey John.
Fear: Hey John.
Doubt: Hey John.
Anxiety: Hey John.
Depression: Hey John.
ME: Uh.... God?
God: Still here.

The Long Surrender

Me: Hey God.

Me: Hey God.

Me: Hey God.

Me: Hey God.

Me: Hey God.

Me:

God: Hey John.

Me: Finally!

God: What's up?

Me: Where have You been?

God: I've been here with you the whole time.

Me: I tried talking to You for hours and I didn't hear Your voice.

God: I was just waiting.

Me: For what?

God: For you to let me get a word in edgeways.

Two Years Of Pouring Paint

As I am finishing up this book, I'm currently celebrating the third anniversary of the "Hey God. Hey John." Facebook page and I'm finding myself dealing with some mixed emotions about it. If I'm honest, I'll admit to you that there have been many days when I wish I didn't have the material to write anything there.

I wish I didn't doubt, but I do. I wish that faith in the unseen came easy to me, but it doesn't. I wish that I never felt abandoned by God, but it still happens. I wish I didn't feel the cold crush of anxiety and depression that can pin me down to my couch and obscure all light, but I still do.

I wish that I could be a happy warrior with a permanent smile while effortlessly quoting C.S. Lewis to the masses. I wish that my relationship with the Divine came easy to me, but it never does. I am still a mess.

A couple days ago I was asked a couple questions for an article somebody is writing about this page. I was asked why I started HGHJ and why I keep doing it?

To the best of my recollection, here is the answer I gave:

I started HGHJ because I had nowhere else to go but to my keyboard. I had run out of ways that I could talk to God. There was no relationship. I was in the midst of the dark night and I felt like my Creator had given up on me. It wasn't that I didn't believe in the existence of God, it was more that I felt like God had decided that I was beyond hope. I sat down at my computer to write my breakup letter to God and then God decided to write back to me.

Why do I continue to write HGHJ? Well, I can answer that in a quick story:

Mike, brother of Monroe

For all of my childhood and for most of my adult life, my parents ran a drugstore that had been in our family for over a hundred years. During that time my dad would often "hire" a number of people who were down on their luck to come and do some odd jobs around the store. Most of the things my dad would have them do were things that any of the full-time employees could have accomplished, but he would constantly keep those tasks open for a person who came in who needed a helping hand.

Of course, over time, word got out in our small community that our store was the place to go if you needed some help. Eventually, with the increased number of people coming in looking for work, our store ran out of odd jobs needing to be done.

At some point, when he couldn't find enough things for people to do around the store, my dad decided that he would start sending people over to our house to help out around our home. On any given day I would come home from school and find a couple guys cleaning out our gutters or shoveling our walk. My father was incredibly trusting and believed everyone is good, a philosophy that often caused chaos.

One morning, when I was a teenager, I remember being woken up in my bedroom by a disheveled, red-haired, wild-eyed young man wearing a one of those beige trench coats you associate with either Inspector Gadget or flashers.

"Your dad says it's time to get up," the man said, as if the whole situation were completely normal.

I sat up bolt upright in my bed, torn between going with a high-pitched scream for help or my usual response to something terrifying of peeing my pants.

"Uh, who are you?" I asked.

"Mike," he replied.

"Uh, Mike?" I asked?

"Yeah, Mike. You know, I'm Monroe's brother."

I had no clue who Monroe was but I figured I better nod like I did if I wanted to make it out of this encounter alive.

"Right. Monroe. Cool..." I said, huddling deeper in the protective cocoon of my Return Of The Jedi comforter.

After another few minutes of abjectly painful small talk, Mike – you know, Monroe's brother – shuffled out my room. I dressed hastily and ran out into our family room to find my dad smiling at me.

"Did you meet Mike?" he asked.

• 506 •

I stared at my father for a couple of seconds before asking him (in what I'm sure was the most respectful tone ever) why he thought it was a good idea to send a complete stranger into the bedroom of his sleeping fifteen-year-old son.

"It was time for you to get up," my dad responded with a grin he couldn't quite hold back. "I hired Mike to paint the roof and I'd like you to help him."

I let out an incredibly loud and dramatic sigh and watched my dad's smile fade quickly.

"Quit whining. Go out to the garage and make sure that Mike found the paint."

I was just about to let out another one of my trademarked barometric-pressure-changing sighs when I noticed something strange happening behind my father. A thin stream of green liquid started pouring down the outside of our window. It started as a dribble and rapidly developed into a torrent of green that covered up three of our six-foot windows facing the backyard.

"Uh, dad, is the color of paint that we are using to paint the roof going to be green by any chance?" I asked.

"Yep. I'm going with bright green this time," he said proudly.

Knowing that I was witnessing something that I would forever remember, I took a quick snapshot in my mind of what I was seeing before I lifted my arm to point out our newly painted windows to my dad.

"I think he found the paint," I said with a grin of my own that I couldn't quite hold back.

My dad turned around and saw the waterfall of green paint pouring down the side of the house and covering up a third and then a fourth window. We ran outside and found Mike (brother of Monroe) standing in the middle of our ranch style roof pouring a giant barrel of green paint everywhere. The paint covered every inch of our roof...and the side of the house... and my dad's garden...and the aforementioned windows... and the hood of my mom's sweet 1984 white Zephyr compact car.

My father let out a slew of cuss words that I had never heard before or since. To this day, I sorely regret that I didn't have a chance to jot down his creative choice of adjectives. It was a flamboyant symphony of swear words that I am sure was on the razor's edge of almost opening up a wormhole between our world and an alien civilization where the F-word was considered sacred.

"What are you doing!?" my dad screamed at Mike, who was just about to crack open a second barrel of green paint to continue his masterpiece.

"I'm painting!" Mike shouted back with a heavily seasoned tone of "duh" to the inflection in his voice.

"Why are you painting like that?" my dad asked, while probably wondering the three thousand ways that my mom was going to freak out when she came home to discover her newly painted everything. My mom had a low tolerance for shenanigans and we were suddenly in the middle of a shenanigan hurricane.

Mike put down the second container of paint and walked over to the side of the roof and stared down at us.

"Because this is the only way that I know how to paint."

My dad's faced relaxed a bit. With the sound of paint plopping off the roof and onto our driveway my dad softly asked, "Can you please stop what you are doing right now?"

Mike, the brother of Monroe, who was now completely covered in the green sludge, looked down at my dad with his painted hands on his hips simply responded with a thoughtful "No."

"Why not?" my dad asked.

"Because I'm not out of paint yet."

* * * * *

I have come to know God in the same manner in which Mike, the brother of Monroe, came to understand painting. Through writing "Hey God. Hey John." I have found a way to pour myself out like a bucket of paint all over the place. At times it can be ugly and it can be messy, but it has all been authentically me. Every word of struggle and suffering that I type is truly what I am feeling at the time of writing it. Each moment I sit down at the computer and hash out the words "Hey God. Hey John." I am being connected to my Creator, because I know that somebody is reading it and that usually they will have something profound to say or share in response. I have come to deepen my relationship with God through all of the people who have shown up to read my conversations. I have learned so much from many different faiths, perspectives and experiences that have been shared with me on the Facebook page.

For those of you who have joined me on "Hey God. Hey John." I want to thank you from the bottom of my heart for giving me hope.

Sure, there are way more efficient ways for me to grapple with and try to understand the mysteries of God, but this has been the only way that has worked for me. I just spill my heart out like paint poured over a roof and hope that it covers everything that needs to be said.

When will I stop writing these conversations?

When I run out of paint.

In Closing

Me: Hey God.

God: Hey John.

Me: Am I on the right path?

God: To what?

Me: Knowing what you want from me?

God: What do you think I want from you?

Me: You want me to be in relationship with You. You want me to be desperate to find You. You want me to serve. You want me to show mercy.

God: Anything else?

Me: You want me to be know how to be happy.

God: I want something far greater for you than just happiness.

Me: Oh, right. You want me to know joy.

God: And...?

Me: Peace.

God: And...?

Me: Hope.

God: Do those answers work for you?

Miss. Millhop: Absolutely!

Me: Whew.

the voice of God
is the loudest
when I am
at my quietest
in the moment
where I find
the strength
to silence my
mind and to
close my
mouth
suddenly
I hear the voice
of God in the
wind above me
and through the
river below me
and through the
people around me
and through the
simmering purpose
within me
the stiller I am
the more God
disturbs me
with a joy
that renders

HEY GOD. HEY JOHN.

me speechless
Hey God
I'm surrendering
I'm ready for You to show
me something
beautiful

Co-Authors

Me: Hey God.

God: Hey John.

Me: I turned all of the conversations we've been having on Facebook into a book!

God: Awesome!

Me: It's all about my journey through my faith crisis and depression.

God: I know, I was right there with you while you were writing it.

Me: Oh, right. You must be really excited.

God: Why?

Me: Because you finally get to be in a book written about You.

God: John...

Afterward

My hope for your empty heart

I know what it's like to exist with an empty heart. I know what it's like to feel as if God has become invisible to you. I know what it's like to find your faith replaced by doubt. I know what it is like to feel hopeless about the future. I know what it is like to scream at the sky for answers and feel unheard. I know the suffering that comes with losing the belief that your life has a purpose. I know what it is like to feel separated from a God to whom you once felt connected.

As a fellow traveller on the road back to faith, here is my advice: be desperate for God. Don't give up on looking for God in places you never thought you would have before. Seek to regrow your relationship with God in a different garden. It could be in the form of daily walks where you can spill your heart out to God. Perhaps you will find a way to include God in your art or your music or in your reading. Or maybe you can rediscover your connection with God through service work and helping others. My belief is that anything can become a prayer if you decide to treat it as sacred.

Try something!

I showed up on Facebook every day and used it as a way to pray to God. I vented my frustrations, doubts and my weaknesses to God and for the first time in decades, I felt heard. What started out as a way of poking fun at my crisis of faith became a vehicle for personal transformation once I allowed myself to treat these dialogues as a form of prayer.

Find a way to reconnect with God. Be desperate. If you no longer feel God in your life like you used to, it may be a sign that it's time to try a new way to pray. The worst thing you can do is to give up on your spirituality when it becomes difficult. God created you out a love that you cannot comprehend. God is waiting on the other side of your doubt to show you something beautiful.

Find a new way to hear the voice of God and allow it inhabit your heart again.

My journey back to a full heart began with a simple:

Me: Hey God.

God: Hey John.

How will your journey begin?

Acknowledgements

This book could not have ever happened without the help and support of so many people. I am forever grateful for the many angels working in my life. Here is the list of those kind souls that I am so grateful for who carried me over the finish line while trying to put this collection together.

To my wife, Jenni, who has been the living embodiment of patience over the past four years while I put my life on hold to have these conversations with God on Facebook.

To my dear friend Gene for his periodic nudges for me to transform these posts into a book. Whenever I had a question, Gene always provided wise counsel. *Anytime I had a problem, yo he solved it!*

To the readers of the Hey God. Hey John. Facebook page. They have been with me from my very first post about waffles and have accompanied me on my wild spiritual rollercoaster. My readers have so generously showed up every day to share their own stories and to lift each other up. To have learned from them has been one of the greatest joys of my life.

To Heidi who edited this project with such kindness and craft. Six months ago I handed her an ever-growing pile of conversations and she so effortlessly helped me sharpen them all into a readable book. I am incredibly grateful to have made a new friend during this publication journey.

To Nelly Murariu at pixbeedesign.com who designed such a lovely cover for my book.

And...

To God, for obvious reasons. I will continue to do the work. I will continue to open my wobbly heart. I will continue to show up to You. I will continue to look for something beautiful every single day.

Chef John's Delicious School Night Curry!

(as promised!)

Ingredients

1¼ pounds boneless, skinless chicken breasts, cut into ¼-inch strips

Salt and freshly ground black pepper

3½ teaspoons curry powder, divided (as a lover of curry, I enjoy higher amounts!)

3 tablespoons vegetable oil, divided

4 garlic cloves, minced and then minced again

2 cups low sodium chicken broth (best quality such as Swanson)

1 tablespoon cornstarch

2 teaspoons sugar

¼ cup whole Greek yogurt (don't use non-fat because why would you?)

A kiss of coconut milk

¼ cup chopped fresh cilantro

Note: I know there are people that like to add peas and onions to their curry but those people are wrong and should just go eat a salad instead.

Instructions

1. Sprinkle the chicken evenly with ¾ teaspoon salt, ¼ teaspoon pepper and 1½ teaspoons curry powder.
2. Heat 1½ tablespoons of oil in a 12-inch skillet over high heat until just smoking.
3. Add the chicken in a single layer and cook, stirring occasionally, until lightly browned but still pink in spots, about 3 minutes. Transfer the partially cooked chicken to a clean bowl and set aside.
4. Add the remaining 1½ tablespoons oil to the skillet and set heat to medium. Stir in the garlic and remaining 2½ teaspoons curry powder and cook until fragrant, about a minute more.
5. Whisk the chicken broth and cornstarch together to dissolve the cornstarch, then add to the skillet along with a ⅛ teaspoon salt. Bring to a boil, then reduce the heat to

medium and cook until the sauce is nicely thickened, about 5 minutes.

6. Add the partially cooked chicken to the skillet, turn the heat down to low and simmer until the chicken is cooked through, a few minutes. Off the heat, stir in the yogurt and cilantro; then season with salt and pepper, to taste.

7. Serve with basmati rice and enjoy!